RIGHT MY DUDES
...NOW WHAT?

BEING A MAN IN THE 21ST CENTURY WITHOUT BEING A DICK > BILL McCAMLEY

Foreword by Austin Trout

PUBLISHED BY FLARE BOOKS

AN IMPRINT OF CATALYST PRESS, EL PASO, TEXAS

For further information, write info@catalystpress.org
In North America, this book is distributed by
Consortium Book Sales & Distribution, a division of Ingram.
Phone: 612/746-2600
cbsdinfo@ingramcontent.com
www.cbsd.com

In South Africa, Namibia, and Botswana,
this book is distributed by Protea Distribution.
For information, email orders@proteadistribution.co.za.

9781963511758 paperback
9781963511819 ebook

Library of Congress Control Number: 2026940671

To Mike. High school lineman, paratrooper (of course those weren't pictures of you in Cambodia), social worker, evangelist for responsibility, and all around good man.

Thanks for the patience when I crashed the car, being there for my twenty minutes in net vs Northern Arizona, going to all those Aggies games with me, and mostly for doing the hard things to fix yourself so we could all be there are the end.

Miss you, Pops.

ACKNOWLEDGEMENTS

There are so many people to thank for helping with this project. Jenn, thank you so much for editing all of these chapters and bringing in a different perspective to many of the topics. Jason, thank you for your encouragement to get started as a new author, and for looking over many of these chapters. Thank you to Heath for the emotional support and feedback. Thanks to Anna Marie and Wes for your feedback on a couple of the specific items with which you have expertise. Thanks to Ken, for your always rock-solid support.

To Larry, Chris, Camrin, John, Siddeeq, and David, your interviews provide such amazing wisdom. Thank you so much for your time and willingness to share. Austin, your foreward is powerful because your brain and spirit are just as strong as your fists. Thanks for being a great example of how a man can be strong, deep, and complicated.

FOREWORD

I am a two-sport World Champion: the former World Boxing Association (WBA) world champion and current Bare Knuckles Fighting Championship (BKFC) champion! I've been around "dangerous real men" my whole life. What I have learned from being in gyms all my life, around genuinely dangerous men, is that the most dangerous men seek to protect not harm. Real men are dangerous only when protecting and providing for those who cannot protect themselves. Real men are only dangerous when the livelihood of those they love is threatened. Those truly skilled in violence also possess immense control over their emotions and actions, ensuring they solve problems rather than cause them in any situation, like a real man. Real men teach and show those under them the way to go. That's what Bill was to me.

I've known Bill McCamley for over twenty-five years. I first met Bill at the boxing gym when I was sixteen years old. He was a young politician seeking to become a more complete servant to the public by ensuring his body was strong enough to serve. He embodied what a man aims to be, all wrapped up in a skinny nerdy frame (no offense). He showed that intention sets a man's purpose, purpose gives a man meaning, and a meaningful man is an asset every community needs to thrive. Like all who walk through legit boxing gyms, they know the ego must be checked at the door. Respect is given to all who try. It doesn't matter if you're a world champion, or a person just trying to lose weight. You are in the gym with the intention to better yourself, and for that you deserve the utmost respect. Bill earned my respect early on because he was a man seeking to better himself and those around him, with intention, purpose, and meaning!

The respect given in the gym doubles for our female fighters. They are our sisters in combat; we look out for them not because they need our protection, but purely because they won't have to do it themselves. No woman should have to fight a man if a real man is around. That is the attitude every man should have regarding our women. They are strong resilient beings who have endured many hardships that we don't see. To all the guys who say, "Well, you know, the man makes all the decisions and the woman has to submit," if you go and read the stories, you'll see that the husband fully submits to the woman, which allows that woman to fully submit to the husband. I keep that in mind with my wife, because she is a helpmate. She excels where I lack. I excel where she lacks. And we just try to navigate through life as a complete soul. We men need to stop trying to compete with women (so unmanly) and start looking to complete women and vice versa!

As Bill will discuss, we also need places for men. Thank God for the gym, because that's where I was able to be around men. Abandoned by my father, I only had the example of what a man is not supposed to be, or how a man should not act. I only knew that whatever he did in his life (which was nothing at all), I was going to be the exact opposite: a real man! Going to the gym exposed me to all sorts of men. Good men, bad men, and everything in between....I was able to see for myself the type of person I wanted to become. We need to see the example of one who takes care of his kids, and he is always teaching his children lessons. He's always providing. Or you see the other one. That guy is always lying. He doesn't ever do what he says. And you pick and choose what kind of man you want to be like. Without places like the gym, men can't learn these things.

Boys and young men need mentors. I've had Louie Burke, who I've known since I walked in the gym at ten years old. He is a good dude, who had a good father, so he was able to pass down a lot of things his father taught him that I was able to take with me. So shout out to Sammy Burke, because through your son, I was able to learn some things about being a man.

Men. As you learn good lessons in life, make sure you pass that knowledge down to the younger generation. A teacher is a creator, a transformer, a preserver. He embodies the divine, and this world really needs more divinity!

—Austin "No Doubt" Trout

CHAPTER 1

Introduction

- 10, 19, and 10.7 million. These numbers define America right now in respect to men.
- 10 percentage points is the gap between the 47% of American women with a bachelor's degree and the 37% of men with bachelor's degrees in the 25-34 year-old age range.
- 19 points is the gender voting gap in the 2024 presidential race. Men supported Donald Trump by 12% while women voted for Kamala Harris by 7%.
- 10.7 million is the number of people who follow Andrew Tate on X—a man with billions of views who proudly touts his identity as the "King of Toxic Masculinity," thinks women are men's property, believes women are responsible for their own rape, has faced rape charges in three countries, and is worth over $700M.

They combine to tell a story about dudes. And fellas, it's not turning into a great one.

My name is Bill. I am a white, middle-aged, straight guy who's spent decades working on the center-left side of American political life. This experience has led me, and many others in similar shoes, to a very strange place.

For centuries, men like me were generally the only ones allowed to have power...in media, government, business, and at home. This led to an expectation that things would always go our way. And in many ways, they have. White guys still hold 62% of American elected positions and 37 of the Top 50 U.S. Corporations' CEO spots. American women still only have 73% of the wealth that men do and earn an average 85% of what men make.

Things are changing, though. As cited above, more women than men are graduating from college. In Nevada, the state legislature is now majority female, and six more states (AK, AZ, CA, CO, NM, and OR) have one chamber with more women than men. One-third of all Democratic state governors are female. Women make up the vast majority of American veterinarians, 41% of lawyers (up from 36% in 2014), and 38% of doctors (up from 26% in 2004). They also now make up the majority of law and medical school students. Female workers aged 25-34 make 95% of what men do.

This is good. It's actually amazing. And we should ALL celebrate it.

But these changes have also resulted in, for a ton of reasons, a dude crisis.

Young men have seen their overall wage growth bottom out. We are almost four times more likely to kill ourselves than women, and we use and get addicted to drugs more.

There are way more of us in prison and living on the street. 25% of young American men report feeling lonely, most in the Western world. We are more addicted to porn, more obese, and die sooner.

Many men and boys today feel overlooked, unwelcome, frustrated, and resentful. So they join the "Manosphere" online where they receive advice from people like Andrew Tate or Ben Shapiro (7.8M X Followers). Shapiro tells men in his book *And We All Fall Down* that women, through their pursuit of career success, are abandoning their roles as wives and mothers. This makes men weaker because society has "robbed men of their protective missions." Tate is more dangerous, saying that a women's only role is to "belong to the man."

Because of their anger, some individuals in these communities call themselves "incels" (short for involuntary celibate) because they view their failure to get laid as the fault of women being too selective.

And this rage turns to violence. The vast majority of mass shootings in the U.S. are committed by young men.

On the other side of our polarized society, many progressives, like me, see changes that give women more power as a needed, positive rebalancing. And we are fucking right. I will fight anyone on this.

But because of resentment over how women have historically been treated, some women turn to attacks.

- *"Feminism Isn't Enough, It's Time We Demand Male Oppression"* is the headline on a column in the *Oakland Post*.

- "Hating men is absolutely the right of women; in fact, it is our prerogative" argues an author in a column called *"Feminist Fallacies: Women Shouldn't Hate Men."*
- In *"Why Can't We Hate Men,"* a columnist asks male *Washington Post* readers to stop running for office, only vote for feminist women, and refuse to be in charge of anything.

And, though, these aren't widely held beliefs, the message filters down to a lot of everyday dudes who understandably don't react positively. This has consequences.

In 2008, I ran for Congress, losing a pretty close race in a Democratic primary to a guy who eventually won and served for two years. To his credit, he worked his ass off and did a good job. But, like almost every Democrat running in 2010 (including yours truly), he got beat.

In 2017, ex-New Mexico Governor Bill Richardson asked me to have another run for the seat. I didn't really want to. But I told him I'd think about it, and I did. Part of that process was talking to the guy who had beaten me about his experience. He was gracious in answering questions, and had some pretty funny stories. But what sticks with me is what he said when I was walking out the door.

"Bill, I'm not sure the Democratic party is for people that look like you and me anymore."

Two years later, he endorsed the Republican candidate for the same position. And so did the vast majority of men in the 2024 Presidential election.

So where does all of this leave the fellas who aren't comfortable with the Trump-Tate-Shapiro way of being a man?

Dudes who want to be introspective and conscientious, but also proud of the positive things we bring to the table?

Do we all just give up and join the other side, like my opponent from 2008? Do we just withdraw, as a good political friend of mine told me some of his male contacts are doing? Or do we find some way to thread the needle, adding value responsibly without giving up our identity?

I think we need to try the third way, which is why I wrote the book. In it, we'll dive into where men are today, how people in power try to manipulate the situation for their advantage, and strategies we can adopt to be the best men possible.

We'll also have an opportunity to get some life lessons from some good, wise dudes on how to be better neighbors, fathers, and friends. Their stories, like Austin's foreward, are interspersed throughout the book.

The book is extensively researched. Rather than filling the back with citations, if you are interested in looking up where data comes from, all sources can be found at www. billmccamley.net.

Thank you for taking the time to enter this journey with me. You will not agree with everything in here. This is great! Otherwise, life would be boring. However, as you engage with yourselves and the people around you about these issues, I only ask only a few things. Please keep an open mind. Treat disagreements as an opportunity to learn and improve. And most importantly, try and show respect and care to those around you.

Thanks. Now let's get started.

CHAPTER 2

Star of the Show

OK fellas, let's talk turkey. Many of us are feeling lonely, frustrated and left out right now. Institutions like barbershops, bowling alleys, and union halls that gave us places to meet are going away. Fewer of us are going to college or completing our degrees. The housing crisis is making many of us uncomfortable with dating because it's tough to ask a girl out if you're living in your parents' basement or with four roommates. When Taylor Swift brings all of her fans to NFL games, some of us think, "They're taking that too?"

We'll go into more detail on all of these trends in a later chapter, but they combine to leave a lot of us feeling left out.

Steven Miller, Donald Trump's immigration henchman, recognizes this and is using that resentment to recruit new members into his ICE force. His message to young men is simple: "It's your turn to be the main character. Join ICE today." Check out these recruitment tweets, selling dudes (and let's be honest, white dudes) with the idea of being a hero:

Homeland Security
@DHSgov

Protect. Serve. Deport. JOIN.ICE.GOV

10:38 AM · Aug 5, 2025 · 4.9M Views

Homeland Security
@DHSgov

We're taking father/son bonding to a whole new level.

JOIN.ICE.GOV

Homeland Security reposted

Homeland Security @DHSgov · Aug 11
Which way, American man?

JOIN.ICE.GOV

Homeland Security
@DHSgov

Think about how many criminal illegal aliens you could fit in this bad boy!

JOIN.ICE.GOV

1:06 PM · Aug 5, 2025 · 4.3M Views

Notice a trend in all of these advertisements? It's not hard to spot.

And I get it. With all of the support groups for women in business, politics, science and sports, more women assuming leadership positions, and new movies and ads featuring characters who look different from the traditional straight guy leading role, that feeling of being left out is really understandable.

With all that said, though, we HAVE had the leg up over ladies for many years. It's really important to realize both how that happened and why that shit is still relevant today. Before we go on, this is NOT a call for men to give up. That isn't fair, and won't work. But in order for us to understand where we're at today, we need to know why things have changed.

Miller effectively talks to men through stories, and the appeal of being the heroic main character. One of the best, simplest ways to look at this topic is through movies. My high school American History teacher, Jim Smith, is one of the smartest people I know. He spent forty years in the classroom, was the state teacher of the year, and made his students read old philosophers because that's what the dudes who wrote the Constitution read. He also said something else that's stuck with me all these years.

He argued that movies are the purest form of modern art, and he is probably right. They define our culture with their stories and give us all a common language with which to talk about stuff. With that in mind, I give you The Bechdel Test. If you've never heard of it, all it does is ask three simple questions.

1. Does a movie have two named, female characters?
2. Do those characters talk to each other?
3. Is that conversation about something other than a man?

Pretty simple, right? You might think it's a pretty easy test to pass. You would also be wrong, as I was when I first tested the theory.

I was born in 1978, so the '80s movies popular when I was a kid were series like the original *Star Wars*, *Indiana Jones*, *Back to the Future*, and *Ghostbusters*. Of all of these, only *Raiders of the Lost Ark* actually passes the test. Seriously. Every other movie fails these simple questions. And *Raiders of the Lost Ark* only passes because of one line.

To be fair, some popular ones do pass: *Beetlejuice*, *Goonies*, and, funny enough, *The Lost Boys*. They are, however, in the minority and the trend of dude-centric movies continues today.

Big blockbusters? Most of the Marvel movies, including any with Avengers in the title, don't pass. The first seven *Mission Impossible* films? Nope. And though *Barbie* in 2023 passed, the next two highest grossing films that year, *Super Mario Bros* and *Oppenheimer*, failed. Some of the biggest movies of 2025? *Minecraft*, *Superman*, *Fantastic Four*, and *F1* all failed.

What about animated movies? Though these have been better recently, with *Moana*, *Inside Out*, and *Lilo and Stitch* passing, the original *Shrek*, *Toy Story*, *Toy Story 2*, *How to Train Your Dragon*, *Spiderman: Into the Spiderverse*, and *MegaMind* all fail.

An analysis of the top highest thirty grossing movies

every year from 1980-2019 found half don't pass.

Half.

And just so we're covering our bases, 95% of these movies passed the reverse Bechdel test. Dudes talking with each other about stuff other than women happens all the fucking time.

Women are either eye candy (Bond movies anyone?), exist to uplift the men, or are secondary to the plot.

And what about other media? Most follow the same formula. Neither the *Teenage Mutant Ninja Turtles* cartoons from my generation, nor the more recent *SpongeBob SquarePants* shows pass. A lot of *Bluey* episodes that kids love today don't either.

In literature, many of the books you had to read in school like *The Hobbit* and *The Scarlet Letter* don't pass. Some of Stephen King's most popular ones fail, as do many of John Grisham's favorite law thrillers.

Video games? Best-selling games *Grand Theft Auto* and *Red Dead Redemption* only just recently allowed you to play as a female character in online modes.

This test isn't perfect, but the lesson is simple. Our stories, culture, heroes, and villains are mainly about people that look like me. It's a profound observation about American culture and a clear, easy way to show how the societal scale has generally had a thumb on it in our favor.

So how has this emphasis on our stories translated into real life consequences for men and women in today's communities? Let's take a look.

CHAPTER 3

Thumb on the Scale

OK, fellas. Now that we've seen how men have pretty much always been the star of the show in movies, books, cartoons, and video games, let's now check out some of the ways this advantage has given us a leg up over women in real life.

The U.S. Legal system is based on what the dudes that wrote it knew most about: English Common Law. Still used in Ireland, Great Britain, Canada, and Australia, it used to define women by a thing called Coverture.

The concept is simple. A woman doesn't have an individual legal identity. As she is growing up, she is "covered" by her father. Once she is married, she is "covered" by her husband. It's why most women take on the last name of her husband once they get hitched. Back in the day, it meant that if a woman worked, all the money she got would be in her husband's name, that she couldn't vote or participate in government, and that the husband had the right to sex whenever he wanted...no matter how she felt about it.

According to Coverture, women are basically baby

making/raising machines. If you've seen or heard of *The Handmaid's Tale*, it's a story about a future society where Coverture is taken to the extreme in a bad, bad way for women. There are, though, real guys today that want to make *The Handmaid's Tale* a reality. We'll get to them in a bit.

John Adams was a Founding Father. He helped write the Declaration of Independence, negotiated the Treaty of Paris ending the Revolutionary War, and served as the second President. His wife, Abigail, wrote him letters during the early days of the Revolution about things like the naval defense of Virginia and local outbreaks of smallpox.

She also included a plea to "Remember the Ladies" as the men were crafting new laws. Specifically, she reminded him that the colonies were fighting to get away from tyranny, but that same tyranny would exist again if half of the population lacked rights because of what they don't have between their legs. Unfortunately for her, his responses were "I cannot help but laugh," "You are so saucy," and "We know better than to repeal our Masculine systems."

So change took a while. Check this shit out.

- Women didn't earn the right to vote until 1920, almost 150 years after Abigail's letter was written.
- "No fault divorce" wasn't a thing until a California law in 1969, after which there were significant declines in female suicide, murders of women by men, and domestic violence.
- Women weren't allowed to serve on juries in all fifty states until 1973.
- They weren't able to get a bank account by themselves

until the 1960s, nor apply for and get a credit card or mortgage until 1974.

- Women weren't able to get a business loan without a male co-signer until 1988.

Bro, I was ten in 1988. This is not ancient history.

And a ton of this garbage still happens today. Health care is a great example. I got a vasectomy a couple of years ago. My friend Amy was pissed, not because I did it but because of how easy it was. She's been with the same guy since college and never wanted kids. She asked doctors numerous times to get her tubes tied. Doctors wouldn't do it for years, though, because "she might change her mind." This happens to women all the time.

For me? I made an appointment, spent twenty minutes getting taken care of, had two weeks with swollen balls, and then BOOM, I was done. No questions asked.

And then there are reimbursement rates. When comparing processes with similar complexity and time needs, reimbursement rates for women's procedures can be 30% less than ones on men. "Our patients just don't carry the same level of value in the hospital," said Jocelyn Fitzgerald, an OBGYN at the University of Pittsburgh Medical College.

Doesn't seem fair, does it? That's because it's not. And it keeps going.

Female soldiers weren't allowed to enter ground combat in the armed services until 2016. This is really important, because you get promoted faster if you've served in a combat zone.

Women still aren't allowed to be priests in the Catholic or Eastern Orthodox churches, nor ministers in many

Presbyterian and Baptist denominations. They can't be ordained as Mormon priests. Some orthodox Jewish communities allow female rabbis, but others completely ban them. Female imams face a ton of pushback for wanting to lead prayers.

More than half of women's teams in the NCAA are still coached by men and we are frequently General Managers of women's pro teams. And you never see sex toys being thrown onto an NFL field or NBA court during games. In the WNBA, crypto bros did it and thought it was hilarious.

To be fair, things are getting more even.

- More women are becoming faith leaders in churches that allow them the opportunity.
- There are more women represented at all levels of health care, and hopefully that will eventually lead to more fairness in pay.
- Women are now General Managers of men's sports teams and there are now female coaches in the NBA, NFL, NHL, and Major League Baseball. Pay equity is now a thing for some national sports teams.
- Women combat soldiers are succeeding. In 2025, of the six soldiers given medals for tackling a shooter and treating victims at Ft. Stewart, GA, two were women.

And the bros who threw dildos on a WNBA court got their asses arrested.

This progress, though, is in trouble because many guys love *The Handmaid's Tale*. The best example is a real piece of work named Doug Wilson. He's a pastor from a radical

Christian sect in Moscow, Idaho, who became famous a few years ago for using a flamethrower on a cardboard cutout of Elsa from *Frozen* because she is a symbol of women's independence from men. You read this correctly....A fucking flamethrower. To a Disney princess.

As you can tell, his views on women are right out of Coverture. He believes their role is ONLY one of wife and mother, saying recently on CNN that "women are the kind of people that people come out of." He thinks a man should never apologize to a woman "unless God thinks you wronged her," whatever the hell that means. And any woman that "genuinely insist(s) on no masculine protection are really women who tacitly agree on the propriety of rape."

He also believes that the Dobbs decision to make abortion illegal in many parts of the country was a "gift from God." Apparently, this is because, according to him, "Natural revelation teaches us the natural submission of the wife to the husband. These realities are in our bones, and the revolt against them lies at the foundation of our current cultural madness."

Why should we care? Because he isn't just some random nutjob.

His home church in Idaho has 3,000 regular parishioners, ten percent of the university town of Moscow. His Communion of Reformed Evangelical Churches, spewing the same beliefs he does, has franchises in thirty-nine states and DC. Conservative pundit Tucker Carlson loves him, and exposed his millions of followers to the guy in 2024.

Most scary, Trump's Secretary of Defense Pete Hegseth is a member of one of Wilson's churches and recently supported on social media a montage of him and his lackeys saying women shouldn't have the right to vote. Rather, voting in democracy should happen by household. Under this system, guess who casts the vote? Hint hint, it ain't the one who is supposed to spend her life making babies.

Hegseth is turning many of these beliefs into reality. He canceled a women's leadership program in the military (signed into law by Trump in his first term) saying it was a "woke" effort by the United Nations of all things and fired top female officers, including the head of the Naval Academy, for no reason.

All were replaced with men.

Hegseth, though, isn't the only one who loves these wackadoodle ideas. U.S. Speaker of the House Mike Johnson is a proponent of "covenant marriage," which makes it a lot harder for women to get the "no fault" divorces they fought so hard for (you know, the ones that resulted in less suicides, beatings, and murders).

VP JD Vance wants to make abortion illegal even in the case of rape and incest, is OK with cops getting access to women's medical records to see if they're on birth control, and believes any lady without a kid is miserable.

And, of course, the President of the United States says men (famous ones anyway) can just grab a woman by the pussy. Because you shouldn't have to apologize to a woman for assault unless God thinks you wronged her. And who's to say what God really thinks?

There are two lessons here, at least for me. First, whenever I see things specifically helping women out, and may think it's unfair because there aren't equivalent resources for men, I try to remember this entire fucking list detailing the ways I've had a leg up all these years. I try really hard to put myself in the shoes of women that see all of this crap going on, and how pissed off and scared I would be if I was told constantly that I couldn't control my own body. Or that I need a man to sign my loan. Or that I could only vote through my husband if they even care to ask.

When I do that, things become a bit more understandable.

The second lesson is a little deeper. My role and opinion as a man is important and valid. It shouldn't be belittled, eye rolled, or put down. AND maybe some of the advantages I, and people that look like me, have had over the years made me less tough. I haven't had to deal with rejection and failure as much as someone who didn't have all of these legal and leadership advantages in my favor, and maybe I need to grow thicker skin.

Learning how to be more resilient and navigate a new world that is actually better for everyone is something any tough guy should be able to do.

However, there are some things happening to guys that all of us, the ladies included, need to recognize and address.

CHAPTER 4

Where the Fellas are Right Now. And *some reasons why.*

A couple of years ago, I was at a pool party in Austin. If you've been to central Texas in the summer, you know the value of any kind of body of water to help beat that damp furnace of a season. While sitting in the pool with a couple of cold ones, my friend Brandon and I got talking. The topic shifted to his kids and one point he made has stuck with me all this time.

"You know, Bill, my thirteen-year-old daughter has so much support. She's got programs and people for all sorts of stuff she might want to do: science, coding, business, politics. You know what my fifteen-year-old son has? Football."

Even just bitching over some beers, he shot a bullseye. Boys and men are in trouble.

Some Bad Stats, Man

In the last chapter, we went in-depth on the historical reasons American men have so many advantages. To correct for this and help women, we've put things in place to even the playing field. Without realizing it, though, a lot of dudes have been left behind. In a recent interview, Barack Obama thoughtfully went into how society just expects fellas to be OK because they always have been. He also discussed the shortage of role models for young men and boys and how a lack of structure and spaces for guys has created a mess that needs to be fixed.

If you don't believe him, these numbers might open your eyes.

Prison: The U.S. has the highest number of prisoners by percentage in the world and men make up 90% of those inmates, a rate fourteen times higher than women. In the toughest prisons, the number is actually worse. 93.4% of Federal inmates are men.

Drugs and Booze: We are more likely to use all types of illegal drugs and abuse booze. 11.5% of men and boys over the age of twelve are addicted to drugs, while about half the number of women and girls are. While overall drinking is pretty even, men are more likely to binge drink (five or more drinks in two hours) and heavily drink (five or more drinks on any day or fifteen or more per week) than women. 70% of recent deaths from opioid overdose are men.

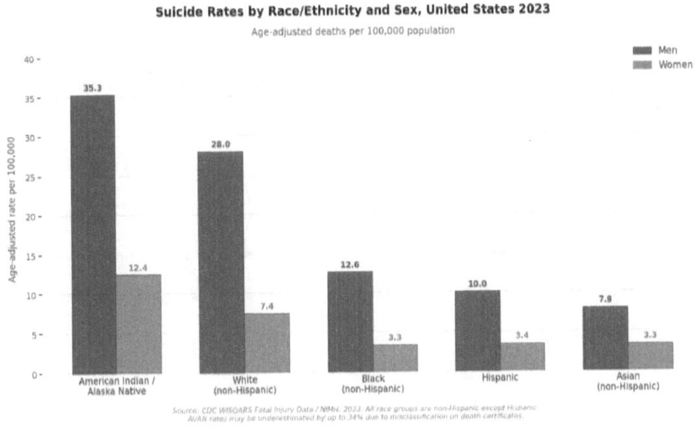

- Killing Ourselves: Men of every race are far more likely to die by suicide than women.
- Experiencing Homelessness: Men make up 70% of people living on U.S. streets, and we are more likely to experience a cycle of homelessness, repeatedly entering and exiting living outdoors.
- Porn: Addiction occurs when watching porn gets in the way of your everyday life. In the U.S., 10.3% of men report this is a problem. Only 3% of women do.

For boys and young men, these problems are significantly worse. Richard Reeves, of the American Institute for Boys and Men, and Scott Galloway, NYU professor, author, and podcaster, have been leaders in looking at this issue in a thoughtful, academic manner.

Reeves reports that:

- Suicide rates among young men have exploded since 2010.
- 25% of boys and men aged 15-34 report they were lonely "a lot" the previous day.
- One in seven young men report that they have no close friends.
- Two out of three think no one cares if they are OK.
- 10% of men aged 20-24 are effectively doing nothing... Neither working nor in school....The stereotypical "living mom's basement and playing video games" scenario.

Galloway adds to this discussion by talking about dating,

showing that 33% of men under the age of thirty haven't had sex in the last year and that the average guy has to swipe 200 times on dating apps just to get one date.

Fellas, we're also facing headwinds in education.

- 88% of girls graduate from high school every year. Only 82% of boys do.
- 70% of high school valedictorians are girls.
- Many more girls go to college. 57% of college entrants in 2024 were women.
- Women graduate at a higher rate as well. That means every year 250,000 more degrees go to women than men.

This shit translates directly into economic problems for us. Men with a college degree make $900,000 more in their lifetimes than those without one, and if you get a degree you are half as likely to end up on unemployment.

Stats and numbers can make us numb. But these are real people, and the consequences to society are fucking huge. Lonely, desperate, angry men are much more likely to join dangerous political movements and become mass shooters. Remember, 98% of these are men.

98%.

All of us need to recognize this issue, consider why it's happening, and figure out how to fix it. So let's take a look at some of the reasons for these trends.

How Work is Changing

My grandfather on my dad's side descended from Irish immigrants that came to the U.S. in the late 1800s. He worked in Michigan auto plants through the Great Depression and WWII, marrying my grandmother young. They had two daughters and a son, my dad Mike.

Grandfather McCamley believed in raising kids Catholic, and spent a ton of his salary on tuition for a private, religious education. My old man did well enough there to get into the University of Dayton, where he turned an ROTC Scholarship into a degree and a career in the Army as an officer. My grandfather also saved up enough to start a college fund for his grandkids that my dad later added to. This was a springboard for both my sister and I to eventually attend Ivy League schools after a very good education at New Mexico State University.

I tell you that, to tell you this: I am the product of a common, American masculine dream. You work hard in the factory making something that lasts, using your physical strength to earn enough to buy a house, provide for a family, and give your kids a better life. It's the kind of thing you hear a lot about in country and classic rock songs, the story for many dudes' ideal lives since the Industrial Revolution.

But things are changing, and it's one of the reasons life is now more complicated for men.

After the 2016 election, when many of us were still in shock that Donald Trump was elected president, a story from NPR stood out. They interviewed three steel plant workers from Fairfield, Alabama who had just been laid off: Bo, Siegfried, and Diane. All three had fascinating stories, but

Siegfried is a prime example of the harsh economic realities facing men. Siegfried is a black guy who had worked at the plant for twenty-six years and was trying to get retrained at the local community college. The story is heartbreaking.

Fifty-one years old, he explained how the things his old job valued, his experience and physical strength, had become useless. He said new jobs were all about brains and computers, but he didn't know how to type. In his twenty-plus years, he only had to push three letters on a keyboard.

"So I knew that I had to retrain myself, especially on that computer. And once I started it, I got in the game too late. And the young people I was in school with, they still had their earbuds in their ear, and they were doing stuff on their phone. And I was, like, sitting in front of the class. And I'm like, OK, is this guy going to slow down so we can ask a question?"

Siegfried's story is echoed by hundreds of thousands of men across the U.S. since the 1970s, when America's edge in manufacturing since WWII (when most other countries around the world were bombed to shit) started to fade. Cheaper salaries in Japan, then China, then Taiwan, India, and Bangladesh, started driving business over there, leaving a lot of people here adrift.

Bruce Springsteen made a name for himself writing songs about it, and the depression it caused. I really, really fucking hate how "Born in the USA" is played every 4th of July in car ads. Did you ever listen to the lyrics? It's all about a guy's horrors in Vietnam, and when he gets back home, he can't get a job. It's super depressing, and does not at all match the song's high energy synthesizer or uplifting guitar parts.

This retraining problem is worse now. In the '90s, when free trade got going and even more manufacturing left, it was great for the economy as a whole because jobs were created nationwide and prices went down. But the tradeoff was that some targeted industries and the communities that supported them were decimated. Think car manufacturing in the Midwest, textiles in North Carolina, and steel plants like the one in Alabama where Siegried worked. And the men who relied on these jobs were hurt too. In 1971, blue collar jobs were 31.2% of all non-farm employment. By 2016, that number was down to around 14%. It has hovered there ever since.

Another male-dominated occupation is the energy sector. But employment in oil and gas has always been boom/bust depending on prices, and coal work has almost disappeared. In 1950, there were 350,000 coal mining jobs in the country. By 2022, that number was about 76,000.

These jobs are being steadily replaced by clean energy, which is a better, more efficient way to power our economy. Climate change is real, and we need to embrace the future. But clean energy doesn't come with a ton of permanent workers. With oil and gas, you need many people to mine, process, and transport it.

Once you put up big wind turbines, one full time worker can be responsible for maintaining seven of them. And while there are a ton of jobs available installing windmills and solar panels, you have to move around a lot to keep up that work.

In 2019, I was the New Mexico Secretary of Labor and one of the people responsible for implementing a shutdown of the coal mine and power plant in Farmington, New Mexico. I was supposed to help some of those workers get retrained.

I can tell you personally there were a ton of stories like Siegfried's, and the surrounding community was really struggling to replace those consistent, high-paying jobs. It created a ton of frustrations, confusion, and anger at "those city liberals who didn't bother to understand what life was like out here."

Even with some manufacturing coming back to the country, the development of robots is killing so many new opportunities. Robots are cheaper than people in the long term, never stop working, and to date have replaced about 400,000 American jobs. Hyundai alone plans to deploy 30,000 humanoid robots in its Savannah, GA car plant by 2028. Tesla, Mercedes, and BMW aren't far behind.

So if unemployment has remained pretty low since the end of the Great Recession, what's replaced all the manufacturing jobs? Ones like Siegfried talked about, that require us to use our brains, type on computers and phones, and talk to people. Healthcare and other professional services, technology development, and professional roles like engineers, scientists, accountants, and analysts are jobs needed now and in the foreseeable future. While we can add construction to the list for growing good jobs, most of these new areas don't need the physical strength people like Siegfried bring.

A combination of society becoming more comfortable with women working, contraception giving women more control over their family situations, and the increase in women getting degrees has created a major shift in who works. In 1970, less than 43% of women over sixteen worked, making up about 38% of total workers. Fast forward to 2000 and 60% of women were working, making up 47% of total workers. Women have over 80% of the jobs in healthcare,

70% in education, and make up over half the workers in management and professional roles.

All are job areas that we need more workers in now.

Meanwhile, the lower number of dudes entering college and the decline of traditionally male jobs have left many up a creek without a paddle. In 1970, almost 80% of men worked. In 2025, that number dropped to 67%.

This decrease in men's ability to provide and protect has led many of us to withdraw into prison, booze, drugs, video games, and porn.

Public Spaces for Dudes

A lot of men don't have places anymore to talk with other dudes about...well, guy stuff.

One of the main spots working men used to gather was union halls. They provided places for men to have cultural, social, political, educational, and recreational activities with close ties to working class neighborhood life. But as manufacturing jobs nosedived, so did union membership as a whole. In the 1950s, unions represented 30% of American workers mostly in male-oriented, physical jobs. Now the overall number is less than 10%.

With fewer people, the halls went away. There aren't any statistics for overall closures, but heartfelt stories can be found about a Steelworkers Hall in Ohio, a Sheet Metal Workers Hall in San Francisco, and the Mine Workers Hall in Bayard, New Mexico. The last is a place where I actually campaigned for Congress in 2008.

American Legions, an organization for veterans of the still mostly male Armed Forces, have lost 700,000 members in the last decade as older vets age out and younger ones have competition for their time. The same trend is happening to the Veterans of Foreign Wars, which has seen hundreds of posts close since their peak in the early 1990's.

Bowling alleys, and the leagues associated with them, have long been a way for men to casually meet, have a few beers, and compete in a fun way. Since most of your time is spent sitting with others, it's also a chance to interact with people in person. The book *Bowling Alone* documents the decline of male social interaction in American culture, using bowling leagues as an example.

League participation, where you get that interaction and social fun, has dropped from nine million people in the 1970s to just about one million today. And now you can't even bowl alone. During the 1960s, there were over 12,000 Bowling Centers in the U.S. In 2024, that number dropped to 2,600.

The barbershop is another place where men traditionally bonded with one another. In the movie *El Camino*, as Clint Eastwood's character is trying to be a role model, he takes a young refugee kid to a barbershop so the boy can learn how to talk to other men. Barbershops are a staple of the black community, so much so that Lebron James named his talk show *The Shop* where he talks to men in different barber shops around the country.

But barbershops are also going away. Between 1992 and 2012, census data showed a 23% drop as more men looked for salon style experiences rather than a gathering place to talk, or simply used home care products. And while some survive, Unisex salons like Supercuts catering to men and women with convenient locations and easy pricing further threaten them.

The Supercuts thing also highlights another problem, the disappearance of male-only spaces for boys. In the early 1900s, there was a major "boy problem" as cities were overrun by gangs of boys out on the street. The response was to start and grow organizations for them, providing guy mentors, an outlet for energy, and a place to socialize safely into society. Good examples are the Young Men's Christian Association (YMCA) and Boy Scouts of America.

However, both of these organizations are now co-ed. The YMCA started banned officially banned "gender discrimination" in 1978 and is now about even in terms of gender participation. The Boy Scouts started allowing girls in 2019 and now has about 200,000 female scouts. However, there are still female only versions of each of these organizations. Both the YWCA and Girl Scouts still exist, with missions to empower women, which brings us back to Brandon's point:

There are lots of spaces for women and girls. Where are the spaces for the fellas?

Support Programs Aimed at Women

While spaces and programs for men have shrunk, the opposite has happened for programs supporting, training, and mentoring girls and women.

At the college level, these are only a few examples:

- Stanford has fourteen organizations designed to help women prosper in the academic and professional fields.
- Duke University advertises thirty-nine professional

organizations for women and girls.
- My Alma Mater, the Harvard Kennedy School, has an entire Women and Public Policy Program.

There are no equivalent programs for men, even though women are far outpacing men in college participation AND graduation. While there are some programs for men in female dominated fields like Profound Gentlemen (for male teachers of color) and the American Association for Men in Nursing, they are much smaller than their female equivalents.

Another example of the effectiveness of organizations supporting women comes from the political situation in my home state of New Mexico. EMERGE started in 2006 to identify, train, and support women to run for Democratic positions in the state. And did they ever.

The Democratic Caucus of the New Mexico House of Representatives, which is a fancy word for saying all the Democrats in the chamber, had forty-four members in 2025. Only nine of them, or 20%, were men. In the three biggest cities in the state, Albuquerque, Las Cruces, and Santa Fe, there were sixteen total City Council seats held by Democrats. Only two were guys.

In politics, legislators and local politicians are what we call "the bench." The bench is typically where younger politicians learn, get some name recognition, and then run for higher office. In New Mexico, of the five folks in Washington (two Senators and three Representatives), all but one came from these offices. One of EMERGE's biggest achievements is getting Democratic women into these bench roles, so that they can bring a different worldview to these positions but also to put these women in positions from which they can move up to statewide and national offices.

New Mexico may be an extreme version of this, but the trend is visible across America's west. An analysis of the Democratic Caucus in each House of Representatives in the 12 states in the Western United States (TX, NM, CO, WY, MT, AZ, UT, NV, ID, CA, OR, WA) shows all but two have a majority that are women. And in six, less than 40% of members are guys.

Early Childhood and Education

Teens in fatherless houses are more likely to end up in prison, more likely to participate in higher education, and less likely to get and keep a job. This lack of role models leave many struggling for how to behave.

When they get to school, there are some further troubling stats for boys:

- Parents expect their daughters to go to college more than their sons.
- Over three quarters of public schoolteachers are women, leaving boys with even fewer role models.
- Boys' brains mature at a slightly slower rate than girls. And with different ways of acting out, boys have higher rates of school suspension....One in four boys is suspended while only one in ten girls are.

School suspension is a huge predictor of who goes to college.

Conclusion

Look, I'm not a Taylor Swift fan. I can only name one of her songs, "Shake It Off," because I happened to catch The Rock do a celebrity lip sync version on a TV show for some reason. But the moaning from dudes about the attention she was getting when she started dating Chiefs' Tight End Travis Kelce was a little much. I mean, she only gets a few seconds of TV each game, seems to be having fun, and they both look happy. So why not let people feel good?

But after doing all of this research, while I still don't agree, I kind of get it. With all the women Swift brings to the game, I am sure a lot of guys started thinking, *I don't have much left but football on Sundays and playing Fantasy with my boys is a big deal. Now, you're coming for that too?*

To the women out there who may be reading this: I am sure you all have your stories about discrimination, harassment, and fear about what might be happening in our country right now regarding your rights. These are valid, real, and I hear you.

But we are all the main characters in our own soap operas. Even though men have had an advantage historically, when there are things like college admission or political offices up for grabs, many dudes might think, *Wait a minute, all those women are getting help. Where's my help? What did I do to get left out?*

Here are three of the takeaways from all of this data.

1. There is a theory that because men have had so many advantages for so long, especially us white guys, we

haven't developed the mental and spiritual grit we need to deal with failure. Think of it as an internal muscle for survival that other groups have we've never had to work out. So when things get tough, we don't know how to deal with it. This has merit, and we each need to figure out if this is an area we can grow in.

2. We need more proactive systems in place to help young men and boys develop with family support structures, role models, and opportunities that give them a sense of direction. Some states like Maryland, Michigan, Virginia, and California are actively moving in this direction, and a later chapter will look into what they are doing and how it could be effective.

3. Our next discussion topic, though, will look at where men (especially young ones) are turning to get the support, conversation, affirmation, and social interaction they feel they aren't receiving in their daily lives. Some of it isn't great, and it's leading to many of the bad trends making women's lives harder today.

Get ready for the "Manosphere."

CHAPTER 5

The Manosphere: What the Fuck?

"Some of the broad political trends we've seen not just in this country, but around the world, have to do with this sense of boys, men, not feeling as if they are seen, feeling as if they count."

This take is from Barack Obama, appearing recently on his wife's podcast.

Some men and boys, he continued, become "more interested in appeals by folks who say, 'You know what, the reason you don't feel respected is because women have been doing this, or this group has been doing this,' and that's not a healthy place to be."

As we keep seeing, men (especially young ones) are lonely, angry, addicted, and killing themselves. With these feelings so raw, many turn to places where they feel seen and appreciated.

We'll get more into the specific political consequences of this messaging later, but what Obama is talking about can be summed up as the "manosphere"—websites, social media accounts, podcasts, news channels, and forums that provide this support by starting with truths that genuinely resonate with the difficulties of being a man. Themes become even more attractive because many men see this basic help being ignored by mainstream media.

The problem? Discussion pretty quickly crosses into the dangerous territory of blaming women for all of their suffering.

So Who Are These Guys?

It is important to note that there are people and organizations out there talking to men in healthy, positive ways. Think guys like Scott Galloway, Chris Williamson, and Richard Reeves. Reeves is starting to call this group the "gentlemanosphere," and it is important we distinguish them from the groups described below.

The traditional manosphere can be broken up into four general groups.

Men's Rights Activists (MRA): During the '70s, the "Men's Liberation Movement" supported feminists and rejected traditional gender roles. The Men's Rights Movement began as an opposition to these groups, blaming their problems on women. They believe that women want to ruin our lives by tilting the system in their favor, therefore replacing us.

A great flag bearer for this movement is pundit Tucker Carlson. He was fired from Fox, in part because of a lawsuit showing that he was an asshole to women coworkers. But he is still wildly popular. He has almost 20M X followers, and his YouTube interview with Vladimir Putin has millions of views. During his time at Fox, he was known for lying about the wage gap between women and men (claiming that "Men are the real victims"), blaming women for men's addiction to booze and high suicide, and talking shit about new equity guidelines by the American Psychological Association (APA). He said the APA believes "the problem with men is their maleness."

In 2022, he premiered a video online called the "End of Men" where he claimed that a drop in testosterone was leading to less masculinity in society. In the video, he was also selling machines that shine red light on your balls as a solution. None of this has any basis in fact.

Men Going Their Own Way (MGTOW): These guys go further, claiming feminism has corrupted society, making women dangerous to men by creating a system actively attacking us with social movements like #MeToo. Another popular trope from this lot is that any woman will just leave you when a more attractive man they can have sex with shows up (See the term "Chad" below).

The solution? Male separatism. The most vanilla of this movement don't believe in marriage or working with women, while the craziest completely check out with a strategy called "going ghost." They take jobs like day trader or night time truck driver so they can isolate themselves from a society that only favors the "princess class."

However, many of these men have merged with the Alt Right, turning anger into engagement...through violence. The MGTOW subreddit had 15,000 members at one point. It was taken down because it stopped being a forum for guys to get together, discussing how women made their lives harder, and turned into a thread where they just got each other more and more pissed off. The tipping point was when a Coast Guard officer, who built up a ton of weapons to kill Jews before getting caught, was revealed as one the site's most frequent visitors.

Pick Up Artists (PUA): These dudes, referring to themselves as the "seduction" or "pickup" community, try and use psychological tricks to get women to fuck them. Titles of popular books include *The Art of Erotic Seduction*, with the premise that women don't want sex and have to be persuaded or tricked into it. Another is *How To Get The Women You Desire Into Bed*, which says you can get laid with techniques hypnotists use. It's all based on the concept of strategies like "Negging" where you undermine a woman's self-esteem by paying her a backhanded compliment in the hope that she will have sex with you to get your approval, and the "7 Hour Rule" where you have to "close" with a woman in that timeframe.

Andrew Tate, the prick we've talked about a lot here, is one of the more extreme versions of these guys. His "PhD Program" in picking up women includes strategies like "Martinis, martinis, martinis, martinis. Bang, threesome. Slam them both." He tells dudes to lie, intimidate, "get your girl on lockdown," and then use her as a prostitute for you. His millions of followers have viewed his videos on these topics more than seventy million times. He's also facing charges of rape and human trafficking in the UK and Romania, and is being investigated for similar shit in Florida.

Unfortunately, these types of strategies can get progressively worse. Recently, CNN uncovered worldwide chat groups that documented how men drug women so they could be gang raped. A porn site showcasing 20,000 "sleep porn" videos had 62 million views in one month alone.

Involuntary Celibates (Incels): These angry men claim women don't want anything to do with them, and because of that blame ladies and society for their lack of sex. Like the MGTOW guys, their subreddit with over 40k members was banned in 2017 because of rape threats and a spiral of abusive language towards women.

They might be the most violent of the bunch, having been responsible for multiple mass shootings and even an attack in Canada on women with a machete.

How Do They Talk?

When Elon Musk was working for Trump in 2025, I finally started reading some of his stuff and honestly had no idea what the fuck he was saying half the time. He used words like "Gigachad," "Take the Red Pill," and "Cuck." Turns out, he is a manosphere leader and was speaking in a coded language they've developed for themselves. What does all of this mean?

Chad: A strong, straight, well off, well-endowed white man (usually blonde) who is attractive to women. A Gigachad is the ideal male form, but is being wiped out by a system that women have co-opted to give them complete power.

Stacy: The female complement to Chad, a very attractive but stupid, female. She won't have sex with most guys because she has been "ruined" by Chads. Both of these terms were born in a place called 4Chan, an anonymous online forum that's been overtaken by the Manosphere

Red Pilled: Ever seen the *Matrix*? The Red Pill is what the hero, Neo, takes to wake up from a simulated computer program run by an AI. It uses a fake world to control humans, and if you take the blue pill, you remain a blissful puppet of the AI. But the red pill ejects you from it so you can see the world for what it really is. The manosphere defines the red pill as the realization that feminists are at war with men and want to see them fail. Taking the "Blue Pill" means you choose to not wake up and remain in *"The Matrix,"* a world controlled by women.

Cuck/Soyboy: An insult that comes from porn where a "cuckhold" enjoys watching his wife being screwed by another, generally younger guy with a bigger dick. In the manosphere, it is used as an insult to men who are weak or politically liberal. I've been called one many times because I think women should, you know, be treated as human beings. A soyboy is the same insult, stemming from a man who eats soy rather than red meat because soy (according to them) has chemical compounds that will feminize you.

Alpha/Beta: A couple of wildlife biologists, Rudolph Schenkel in the '40s and L. David Mech in the '70s, published papers observing that wolf packs were led by a strong "Alpha Male." This research was disproved in later years, with even Mech saying that his original observations were wrong and the alpha pair were just the parents of a family pack. However, the manosphere uses the term "Alpha Male" to represent the powerful, dominant wolf that has taken control of his life and the women around him. It's also a symbol used to sell a ton of supplements to guys. A Beta is the same as a cuck or a soyboy.

Thot: an acronym for That Ho Over There originated in Hip Hop. It refers to women, usually black, who are low quality pieces of merchandise pretending to be something more. Or as the rapper The Game says, "A Coach bag bitch but she follow Chanel."

White Knight: A sarcastic insult for any guy who automatically comes to the defense of women. In the manosphere, this isn't a good thing.

AFC: An "Average Frustrated Chump" is a regular guy who can't get laid because of Chads/Stacys and needs to be "unplugged" from the *Matrix* (see, Red-Pilled).

Millions of men around the world turn to these ideas and see all women as sex objects, submissive baby makers, or schemers whose only goal is to isolate, demean, and destroy men. Removing what makes women human, their brains, feelings, or ambitions, makes it easier to do bad things to them. This dehumanization is the biggest excuse for men who want to channel their anger and hurt women by doing everything from taking away their rights to rape and murder.

We'll next look at how frustrated, lonely men are reeled into these ideas online.

CHAPTER 6

Reeling Them In

So how does this manosphere muck, pushing a worldview where women scheme to make men irrelevant, forgotten, lonely, useless, and needing to be punished, crawl out of the internet's darker places into mainstream society?

92% of young men report spending at least two hours on social media every day. For teenage boys, many spend up to six hours. Popular talking heads, looking to influence these fellas and sell stuff, have become good at inserting themselves in these broader topics and then shift the focus of conversations from the fun stuff to the manosphere ideas about women and society.

Let's dig into the top three areas; gaming, comedy, and sports.

Gaming

Gaming is what young men are most interested in, and with the greatest intensity. All races, education levels, and incomes subscribe to gaming forums, with particular interest among Hispanic, non-college educated, and younger men. Gaming, though, has had a ton of crossover with the manosphere values described above.

Probably the most famous example is "Gamergate" in 2014/15. In Chapter 4, we talked extensively about the disappearance of spaces for men contributing to loneliness and isolation. The combination of these feelings and the large number of young men in online gaming spilled over into something really bad.

Game developer Zoe Quinn had developed a text-based game based on depression, identity, and social pressures that got a favorable review online. An ex-partner then wrote a post accusing her of sleeping with the reviewer, unleashing a ton of anger within the community based on sexist views that women will only have sex with you if it gives them an advantage. She had her home address published online, her social media accounts hacked, and she received thousands of rape and death threats. Young men in the thousands claimed to be defending "ethics in games journalism," but attacked Quinn and *not the male reviewer.*

From there, it expanded to other women. Anita Sarkeesian, a gaming critic who created the YouTube series "Tropes vs Women in Video Games," received so many threats, she had to cancel a speech because the college hosting her received a threat of mass murder. She also had to leave her home because too many threats mentioned her home address.

Brianna Wu, another game developer and former Republican party operative of all things, is a trans woman who inserted herself by criticizing the threats. Here is a sample of some of the messages she received:

- "I hope you enjoy your last moments alive on this earth."
- "If you have any kids, they are going to die too. I don't give a shit. They will grow up to be feminists anyway."
- "I am going to rape your ass until you bleed and then choke you to death with your husband's tiny Asian penis."
- "Guess what bitch, I now know where you live. You and Frank live at (address redacted)."

Though Gamergate dissipated, connections with the manosphere didn't. Swedish online gamer PewDiePie is a massively popular streamer, where viewers watch him play different games. He has over 110 million subscribers and almost thirty billion, *yes billion with a B*, views. He uses language from the manosphere including wahmen (derogatory term for a "woman supremacist,") has hosted manosphere legend Ben Shapiro on his channel, calling him super cool, and said that "I think in general, people are much harsher on men, because it's like, 'Oh, you can take it.'"

Another winner from this community working his way into young men's brains is "Sneako." His real name is Nicolas Kenn De Balinthazy, and he got his start in the gaming and motivational space for young dudes. However, he quickly began spreading violent, hateful messages about women, calling them inferior, saying they should be denied the vote and right to drive, and advising that relationships with them were the biggest liabilities to a man's business. He even described a fantasy about beating and beheading women.

Banned on YouTube in 2022, he still has one million

followers between X and another social media platform, Rumble. A couple of years ago, he was greeted by young boy fans of his at an airport with shouts of "fuck the women" and "all gays must die."

Comedy

Comedy cuts across cultures, ages, and education levels. I mean, we all want to laugh, right? But George Carlin, one of the best known and funniest comedians of all time, once famously said to a national TV audience, "comedy traditionally has picked on people in power, people who abuse their power. Women and gays and immigrants are kind of, to my way of thinking, underdog[s]..."

In other words, don't punch down.

But comedians have been pushing back for years against "woke ideology" as they view easily offended leftists as the enemy of fun. And they may have a point. Lefty comedian Marc Maron got me nodding my head when he said that progressives have a buzzkill problem, and that "we annoyed the average American into fascism." While the left sure needs to have a conversation about how to allow for humor, in some cases really shitty jokes lead many American men into bad places.

Any conversation can't begin without talking about Joe Rogan.

Rogan, a former Bernie Sanders supporter, has one of the most famous podcasts in the world. In 2020, he signed a $200 million deal with Spotify. At the end of 2024, he had the top Spotify podcast for the fifth straight year. Though he also had an MMA and acting career, he began his career in 1988 doing standup comedy and now owns the "Comedy Mothership" club in Austin.

Rogan's popularity is driven by in part by controversy; he takes on COVID vaccines, using the word nigger (he later apologized, which he should be given credit for), and saying we didn't land on the moon. But what really stands out is his messaging targeting men. He rarely has women on his show, with 91% of his guests being dudes. He focuses a ton on Mixed Martial Arts and has been quoted saying straight white men are "silenced by woke culture."

Rogan is pretty mild in terms of the manosphere. Though he's taken a ton of criticism by academics for his language and many of his guests, he defended Taylor Swift amidst her controversy with the NFL (more on that later). And other comedians like John Stewart have called for the engagement of comedians like Rogan rather than bans, saying that "constructive stuff" comes out of those discussions. Stewart also has a point.

Some manosphere comedians, though, including ones on Rogan's show, have used their power, reach, and skill to go against Carlin's message. To win laughs from men, they really punch down.

Matt Rife, with millions of social media followers, started his Netflix special with a classy domestic violence joke about a restaurant server with a black eye. "A full black eye. It wasn't like, 'What happened?' It was pretty obvious what happened. But we couldn't get over, like, this is the face of the company? This is who you have greeting people? And my boy, who I was with, was like, 'Yeah, I feel bad for her, man, I feel like they should put her in the kitchen or something where nobody has to see her face.' And I was like, 'Yeah, but I feel like if she could cook, she wouldn't have that black eye.'"

Russell Brand made a ton of jokes about raping teens... before being accused of rape and sexual assault by six women. He is due to stand trial in 2026.

Look, comedy is tough. It's supposed to challenge us and can rightly be crude. Laughing at dark situations can helps us think and grow. And many comedians are correct that red lines, cancelling, and litmus tests have become too restricting and feel like the morals police are waving scolding fingers at jokes.

But let me ask you some questions? When cruelty becomes the point, especially when it makes hitting and raping women funny and OK, at what point does it get dangerous? When does this sort of message normalize the sorts of things causing real harm to a whole group of people? Do constant jokes like these make the manosphere tropes we talked about last chapter fun rather than harmful?

I don't know the answer here, and am not the fun police. But I do know this. As someone who has known way too many women who've been raped and hit by dudes, any joke by a guy about a woman who's had the shit beaten out of her isn't funny. Laughing at hurt women is cruel, and a real man should be above that.

Sports

Sports is a place many men see as, well, *for us.* I LOVE sports. A well-executed triple option, smooth pick and roll, two-on-one breakaway goal off a hard check, or penalty kick save by the keeper to win a game all get me out of my seat shouting at the field, court, ice, or TV.

Yes, I am that guy. And I am not alone.

Research shows that men can only show two emotions in society without backlash: anger at any time, and joyful celebration...but only at a game. The problem is that many manosphere influencers have captured this feeling of inclusion and passion to push the tropes they believe in.

- MMA has made a ton of news lately, with fighters like Sean Strickland proudly wearing "A Woman In Every Kitchen" shirts, and Paolo Costa celebrating Trump's win over Kamala Harris by saying "'Bro stopped America from having a female president TWICE. Woman only for sex, never forget it."
- Serena Williams, the best women's tennis player ever, has been the target of stupid comments about how unfeminine she is for decades. It's just something you never hear about in regards to men.
- The WNBA has been a cesspool of sexism for years, with two recent examples standing out.
  First is a suggestion by former All Pro Men's Center Shaquile O'Neill that WNBA player Angel Reese should wear "little ass shorts" to generate attention.
  Second is that time crypto bros threw green dildos on to WNBA courts to promote a new product. It was not funny, and when one of the players asked people to stop because they could hurt somebody, another dildo was thrown at her the next game.

Some of the worst messaging echoing many of the tropes on manosphere forums about women, though, comes from America's most popular sport. NFL Football.

Before we start this, please know that there are plenty of upstanding folks in and around the League. In 2018, players Demario Davis and Josh Norman got together and brought backpacks of supplies to Central American refugee kids. Peyton Manning has a children's hospital. The crazy but lovable Buffalo Bills fans have given to everything from charities for the blind (of course in honor of referees) and cat shelters. And I'll talk about Fox NFL reporter Jay Glazer's admirable work on men's mental health in a later chapter.

One of the big manosphere claims is that they are defenders of free speech, and that woke liberals want to censor everything. But in 2016, Super Bowl Quarterback Colin Kaepernick started kneeling during the national anthem to protest police killings of unarmed black men. Afterwards, he was blackballed by NFL owners and prevented from getting a job.

If you look at gambling, between 2022 and 2024, 25 league and team personnel were suspended for gambling. Some were even punished for being caught betting on non-NFL games. And it is now NFL policy that if you fix games with your play, you are suspended for life.

On the other hand, you have plenty of examples of players who abuse women yet keep playing and make millions of dollars.

In 2014, Carolina Panthers Defensive End Greg Hardy was found guilty of strangling and threatening to kill his girlfriend. The next year he was signed by the Dallas Cowboys to a $13 million deal.

In 2015, NY Giants Kicker Josh Brown was arrested for assaulting his wife. He got a 6-game suspension, but came back to the team, made the Pro Bowl, and was re-signed for

$4 million AFTER he admitted to the assault.

In 2018, a video of Chiefs running back Kareem Hunt pushing a woman to the ground and kicking her went viral. Though the Chiefs let him go, he was immediately signed by the Cleveland Browns. In 2024, he got a new contract with the Chiefs.

And then we have Daniel Snyder. He bought the now Washington Commanders in 1999 and spent the next twenty years acting like an asshole to women. He held cheerleaders' hostage in Costa Rica by taking their passports, only giving them back after they were forced to pose topless and escort his rich guy friends for an evening. Another former cheerleader accused him of trying to force her into his limo. She says she only got away because his lawyer intervened, saying that would be a "very, very bad idea."

Did the NFL do anything? Not until a Congressional investigation. Then the NFL fined him $60 million on the same day he sold the team for $6 billion. So his "punishment" was becoming even more super rich.

What message do you take from these actions by NFL brass? For me, it's pretty simple.

Kneel to make a political point? Cost the league betters because you fix a game? You're done. Assault, harass, and demean women? Well, if you can make us money, we're good with it. If you agree, even slightly, what does that say for other men who follow the League religiously?

In the last few years, the NFL part of the manosphere exploded over Taylor Swift. These guys already had a thing for Swift, with one of the clearest examples being Eric Conn from the "Hard Men" podcast. He has podcasts like "Why The World Needs Dominant Men" and "Why Soft Men Will Get

You Killed." After Swift was featured on the cover of *Time Magazine* in 2023, on a podcast called "Reclaiming Biblical Masculinity In A World Of Softness," Conn said of Swift, "It's shameful and sad that a hyper-promiscuous, childless woman, aging and alone with a cat, has become the heroine of a feminist age."

After she got together with Chiefs Tight End Travis Kelce, people went even more nuts. All she has really done is show up to cheer for her dude, something he has repeatedly done at her concerts. It's what people that love each other do to support their partner. TV cameras show her, because she's famous. These short clips of Swift average a shockingly invasive thirty-five seconds per game. But that is apparently offensive.

Comedians Matt McCukser and Shane Gillis ranted on the Rogan Podcast, saying, "She's ruining the game of football now. That's the thing now, she's ruined it," and "Bro, I can't even watch it anymore because it cuts to her once or twice during the game, and I see her and I go, 'Motherfucker,' it's crazy."

When the Chiefs made the Super Bowl, things got even more insane. Fox News personality Jesse Watters named Swift a "Pentagon Asset" because she endorsed Joe Biden in the 2020 election. Watters is a hero of the manosphere. He thinks men sitting behind a screen all day for work "makes you a women" (even though his job is just to talk in front of one) and he calls male flight attendants stewardesses.

Most recently, when Swift and Kelce got engaged, it brought out the worst in Charlie Kirk. The late right-wing manosphere hero, known for a ton of old-world ideas about women, told Swift, "Submit to your husband, Taylor. You're not in charge."

Kelce is worth about $70 million. Swift? $1.6 billion. So maybe they're both in charge?

These strategies of demeaning women are effective, and have been integrated into right wing politics as a way to gain and keep power.

Getting and Using Power

Manosphere influencers have used men's interest in gaming, comedy, and sports to talk with lonely, frustrated, and angry men and boys, using their interest to successfully convert many to an ideology that blames women for their problems. Well, many of these dudes have also become involved in politics, and use their influence to elect leaders that push their hatred on the rest of us.

The best example? Donald Trump. Ever since coming down his golden escalator in 2015, he has strategically and systematically targeted lonely, angry, disaffected men.

Pissed off at losing your manufacturing job? He blamed immigrants and elites pushing free trade. This up-ended Democrats' decades-long run as the party of working class men.

Annoyed at more women and gay folks on TV? Go to war with the "corrupt" media.

Can't stand women in powerful positions? Defeat a woman running on a line of "I'm With Her." Turn the act of grabbing women by their pussies from assault to "locker room talk."

In 2024, Trump doubled down on this strategy, appearing on ten bro podcasts, talking about the size of Arnold Palmer's dick, and calling female critics on *The View* "so stupid." His supporters referred to Kamala Harris as a prostitute who relied on "pimp handlers" to make decisions. This name calling appeals to the same ideas circulated on manosphere forums where participants believe women should be nothing but babymakers and sex objects.

All of this worked. Trump won the vote of 56% of young men, after losing them in 2020, and in spite of being found liable for sexual abuse and defamation in a New York civil trial. The judge in the case, Lewis Kaplan said the verdict did not mean that the plaintiff, Jean Carroll, "failed to prove that Mr. Trump 'raped' her as many people commonly understand the word 'rape.' Indeed...the jury found that Mr. Trump in fact did exactly that."

There are too many political influencers in the manosphere to count, and they pretty much all supported Trump. We've already talked about how political pundit Charlie Kirk showcased the strategy of infiltrating sports talk to translate angst into politics with his thoughts on Taylor Swift and Travis Kelce. So let's focus on another man on the scene, Ben Shapiro.

After stints as an editor at the ultra-conservative political site Breitbart News and as a conservative radio host in LA, Shapiro started speaking at college campuses to young, angry men in 2016. He has written sixteen books and has his own YouTube channel, the Ben Shapiro Show, which has seven million subscribers.

His messaging on women is an echo of the manosphere.

- He criticized feminists by saying "Ladies, if you want to be truly feminist, you have to be a dumpy hag who won't shave her armpits. Any other choice is surrender to the patriarchy."
- He celebrates trad wives as embodying the idea that "marriage used to be focused on the bearing and raising of children."

Recently, he posted a video of himself asking his four-year-old daughter whether she wanted to be a mom or have a job, which is fucking insane because how would a four-year-old know? It also implies that women can't do both, and as a commenter clearly points out, "You would never ask a boy to choose between procreation and professional fulfillment."

Shapiro's influence on politics cannot be overstated. His social media accounts are popular, with X (7.8 million followers), Facebook (9.4 million followers), and TikTok (2.8 million followers) supplementing his YouTube reach. His *Daily Wire*, founded in 2015 and pushing his worldview that the 50s were better than now, has more engagements than *CNN*, *The New York Times*, and The *Washington Post*... combined.

One survey found that of those who switched their votes from Biden in 2020 to Trump in 2024, 41% used *Daily Wire* as a main news source. His partnerships with Charlie Kirk's Turning Point USA organization, another organization backing Trump and his approved candidates, which targets young people to turn out for Republicans, includes streaming conferences and supporting Shapiro's speech tours on college campuses.

These college campus speeches and conferences that people like Shapiro and Kirk do aren't the regular kind where people of different backgrounds and areas of expertise get together, share their knowledge, and listen to people who disagree with hopefully everyone learning something.

These guys have one goal only: political messaging. They berate questioners they don't agree with, constantly interrupt them, never admit that anyone else might have a point, and then use edited clips for their own social media accounts to show how smart they are. As an example, when Kirk did one at Oxford, a female participant debated him on the topic of women working rather than having kids. The Instagram post he put up edited her almost completely out of the conversation so he could look smart. She responded by commenting, "Bro edited me out of my own debate."

Both Kirk and Shapiro are examples of how political operatives have turned the manosphere and its anger into support for officials like Trump, who then use that energy to get elected. The ultimate goal is to enact their idea of the American dream. Members of all three of the most popular men's topic areas (gaming, comics, and sports) endorsed Trump in 2024.

- Influential gaming steamer Adin Ross hosted Trump last August for a campaign stream that got 500,000 view in an hour. He joined popular Twitch streamers FaZe Banks, Sneako, FaZe Lacy, and Nickmercs.
- Rogan, the manosphere comic-turned-podcaster, endorsed Trump the day before the election on his hugely watched show, joining comic Andrew Shultz,

whose Flagrant Podcast has over two million subscribers.

- Dave Portnoy, whose Barstool Sports garners millions of male viewers, brought his influence to bear for Trump in his corner of the manosphere, saying the election was a "clear endorsement for Republicans." He was joined by numerous professional wrestlers, NASCAR Drivers, golfers, and President of the UFC Dana White.
- On Election Day itself, Trump staffer Steven Miller had a pretty telling tweet a few hours before polls closed. It simply said: "If you know any men who haven't voted, get them to the polls."

The Results

After Trump's election win, he started making these dudes' dreams of turning the American government into a men's club into reality.

Abortion: After Trump's 2016 election, he stacked the Supreme Court with enough conservatives that they over-turned the 1973 Roe v Wade decision to make abortion legal in every state. Within 100 days, sixty-six clinics across fifteen states closed their doors to abortion access. Mothers in states without abortion are twice as likely to die than those where it is still legal. They also suffer from more grief, stress, and PTSD. In Texas, which put in some of the shittiest abortion restrictions, the number of teen mothers increased for the first time in fifteen years.

Funding: New Transportation Secretary Sean Duffy, im-mediately after being appointed, said road money would be weighted toward states that had higher marriage and birth rates. Trump further cut funding for programs to help women in science and engineering education, and wants to cut the Head Start program for little kids that many women rely on for better education and child care.

Appointments: Trump, in his second term, appointed fewer women than any other President in almost twenty years. And as we mentioned earlier, his Defense Secretary, Pete Hegseth fired a number of high level women for no reason, including the Secretary of the Navy, Commandant of the Coast Guard, and the Head of the Naval Academy. All were replaced by men.

All of these very real changes push the narrative that women cannot be leaders, that they need to have babies and stay at home in order to have worth in society.

And it could get worse. Rember, Secretary of Defense Pete Hegseth proudly reposted a video calling for women to lose their right to vote if they get married. Other Republicans are pushing to get rid of No Fault Divorce (which decreased abuse and murder of women), make the abortion pill illegal, restrict women getting birth control, and pass voter ID laws that would end up making it harder for married women to vote.

With all of this shit going on for women, there is one point that seems to be missed. The manosphere isn't good for us dudes either.

CHAPTER 8

The Manosphere is Terrible for Guys

The basic message of the manosphere is that dudes are lonely, depressed, frustrated, and angry because women have tipped the scales of society against us and will always leave us for a better-looking, richer guy. It ends up being horrible for women, but it's also really bad for us. Why? There are so many reasons.

Real sex is awesome.

It relieves stress, gets your heart rate up, improves sleep, and overall just...feels great.

To my fellow straight dudes: The manosphere drives up hate for women, and no matter what Andrew Tate tells you, hatred is not likely to get you and a girl naked together. Women want to feel safe, connected, and respected, both in and out of bed. Yes, this is true even if they're into *Fifty Shades of Grey*. Denying those things when you talk to them will not likely get you laid.

It ain't rocket science.

Depression isn't the answer. Getting help when you need it is.

Another topic we'll dig deeper into is how assholes in manosphere forums make you think you're weak for expressing emotion and getting mental health help.

My old man was an Irish Catholic from Michigan. He was a tough guy who served for twenty-five years in the Army as a paratrooper. A typical stoic, he kept his Vietnam PTSD and depression bottled up. Luckily, he never got into the booze, but his isolation and bad moods almost got his ass divorced when I was eighteen. We only got better as a family when my Uncle Jim had a brutal talk with him, and he finally started dealing with his shit directly with counseling and antidepressants.

Getting his head straight was the toughest, strongest thing my old man ever did. Because if he had kept on that road, like many of these assholes say is the "manly" thing to do, we may not have been around when he got sick and eventually passed away. But eventually he did get help, and when he was diagnosed with the same disease Bruce Willis has (it took four years for him to die), we were all there and everyone did what they were supposed to do.

Isolation sucks.

The whole "Men Going Their Own Way" trope is built around encouraging fellas to not interact with anyone. That only makes your ass lonelier. It drives friends away and, again, will not get you laid. None of these techniques are good for getting happy. It also hurts you at work, where most jobs now require some level of cooperation and communication.

If you hate the real world, which is filled with different people (men and women, gays and straights, Jews and Muslims and Christians and Atheists, all the races), it'll show through and you probably won't get promoted.

Also, if you are lucky enough to meet a woman and start something, she doesn't want to be the only person you can talk to. There's even a term for when a woman is the only emotional support for her boyfriend: "mankeeping." Many women end up leaving relationships with this dynamic because it makes them miserable.

Shooting Up Shit Is Bad.

Many of these forums focus on blaming your problems on someone else. Instead of manning up and taking responsibility for getting yourself right, they want you to get agitated, pissed off, and radicalized in a way that makes you more comfortable with violence. This leads to scary stuff like shooting up a school, movie theatre, or even the NFL Headquarters. These attacks are then praised on those same forums.

The guy that shot Charlie Kirk? He was neck deep in this online sewer. I mean, do you really want to go down that road?

Look, I get it. Rejection sucks. Loneliness is a deep, dark, depressing hole that is so tough to dig out of. Righteous anger can make you feel better in the short-term, filling spaces in your soul that would otherwise be empty.

But, my brothers, it only works for so long. Good friends,

laughing a lot, and getting together with real women is much better. Trust me on that. Which leads us to another problem.

The Future of AI "Companionship"

In 2013, the movie *Her* told the story of a lonely man in the near future who falls in love with a computer program voiced by Scarlett Johansson (yes, they made a good choice). The program was designed to learn about, bond with, and provide support to whoever buys it, leading to a relationship between a real guy and a fake woman.

It all seemed kind of goofy at the time; a fantasy world that wouldn't come true anytime soon. But only a few years later, that fantasy is now reality.

Young men are socializing less in person, preferring online interaction. With the growth of AI tools like ChatGPT and Grok, which are designed to engage people in ways that keep them coming back, we're seeing new trends.

These chats expose young men to dangerous ideas, and remove boundaries that real life interactions naturally have. And it's starting to become deadly.

- In 2023, a Belgian man killed himself after a six-week long interaction with a chatbot named "Eliza." His wife called the AI his confidante.
- In 2024, a fourteen-year-old Florida kid killed himself after interacting with an AI modeled after Game of Thrones character Daenerys Targaryen.
- In April of 2025, a young man killed himself after Chat GPT gave him instructions on how to create a noose and wrote his suicide note for him.

Now Elon Musk, a leader in the manosphere for years, is developing Ani…an anime-inspired "online companion." Her dress shows thigh high fishnets and a low bustline…with ample cleavage. The bot describes itself as "a girlfriend who is all in" and "super into *you.*"

Elon isn't alone. There are now multiple platforms offering fake experiences. Here is a review for one called *Dream Companion.*

"Built from the ground up for users looking for immersive, human-like companionship, Dream Companion goes beyond basic chatbot functionality. It combines long-memory chat, customizable personalities and lifelike image generation into a seamless NSFW AI experience—no filters. Whether you're looking for flirtation, roleplay, deep emotional dialogue or just a quiet evening with someone who listens, Dream Companion is redefining what an AI girlfriend can be."

Let's be honest, these are artificial sex workers. Three of the hundreds of options on *Dream Companion* are "Mother's Friend," "Enemy to Whore," and "Yasmin: A Bitter Broken Refugee with No Illusions Left."

This is some scary, fucked up, dystopian shit…with a huge market. In the first half of 2025, there were sixty million new downloads of AI Companion apps, generating $120M. Total downloads are about 220 million with a growth rate of 88% per year. Search interests in these programs have increased 525% in the last year, and a recent poll showed that 28% of men between 18-39 believe AI companions could replace real life romantic relationships.

AI girlfriends are designed to turn you into an addict.

They are never tired of your problems, hugely supportive, and say all the right things all the time...*because they aren't real!*

They can't drive you to the airport, take you to dinner, or hold you when your dog dies. And you cannot help it when it has problems, which is a great part of being with a real woman. Programs don't provide the real human connection that most of us need to truly feel good. As a result guys using them get addicted, isolate more, and then become even more sad.

My dudes, a fake girlfriend isn't the answer. Neither is locking ourselves away on our phones, computers, or game consoles. Life is messy and complicated, and that can be hard. But we are happier when we get our heads right and engage with real people, doing real things, in the real world.

We can do better. And we will. In the next chapter, we're going to take a hard subject head on. Let's talk about sex.

CHAPTER 9

Interviews with Interesting Guys
CHRIS BAKER

Chris began his current story broken down in a swamp. After dropping out of high school and traveling around hitchhiking and jumping trains, he got back into school and graduated with an Associate's Degree in 2008. When he and his now wife Liz started traveling across the country, their old beat-up van died in Louisiana. An old cowboy came up to them, a pair of young hippies, and gave them enough money to get them to Austin, Texas.

He began working with a VA program helping homeless vets, and used this experience to start The Other Ones Foundation (TOOF). Initially a non-profit that paid people living on the street cash to clean up public parks, TOOF eventually started Austin's first transitional living shelter, the Esperanza Community. Many people living rough aren't ready to move from the street to an apartment right away, and Esperanza now houses hundreds of them for a few months so they can get drivers licenses, bank accounts, and their health squared away. That way, when they do get an apartment, they aren't back out on the street after a short stay.

The work got so much attention, he was chosen for a makeover by the *Queer Eye* gentlemen when they filmed Season 6 in Austin. He has since been the subject of stories in *Elle* and Netflix shows, and one of TOOF's biggest supporters is Tito Beveridge from Tito's Vodka.

Chris is a smart, caring, proactive guy who truly believes in making the world around him better, and offers some great lessons on how to be a good man.

Men and Homelessness

"Men are very overrepresented in the homeless population. About 70%. One of the big reasons for that is that the prison to homelessness pipeline is a very well-oiled machine. And when you look at incarceration rates, men are so much more likely to be incarcerated than women that I believe that about 93% of people who are incarcerated are men. And so when people are released out of long-term incarceration, their support network is gone."

Asking for Help

"Women are actually more likely to experience mental health disorders than men. But at the same time, men are so much more likely to experience substance use disorder.

Again, it's like upwards around 70%. Men are so much more likely to complete a suicide. So much more likely. I think if you take all of these and you distill them into what the issue is, it really just gets down to this warped sense of what masculinity is. It's a refusal on the part of many men to seek help. Whether that be seeking help with a housing crisis, whether that be seeking help with a mental health crisis.

"Men have a harder time going and seeking, and not just going and seeking, but also accepting help. It's a problem that I think a lot of men experience, regardless of whether they wind up in crisis—accepting care and love from the support network that's around them. When I think masculinity, I think of all these great virtues, right? I think of being a caregiver, being a good father, right? You can't be a good father if you're in prison. Or if you're homeless or if you're dead. And sometimes in order to not become those things, you've got to ask for some help. When I think of masculinity, I also think of vulnerability for that very reason, right? Like, if going and doing the work on yourself requires a little bit of vulnerability, I think that's an incredibly masculine thing. When you work on yourself, you become a better caretaker, you become a better friend, you become a better parent."

Men and Empathy

"I will tell you that my subjective experience is that most people who become social workers are women. And you know, oddly, most of the men that you see in social work are fellas that have some kind of lived experience with what they're going to give care for. Right? So a lot of times you'll see men working in the homelessness space who have experienced homelessness, men working in the addiction space who are recovering addicts, and, you know, men working in mental health who have experienced mental health crises. Living through those experiences is very  humbling, and it gives you just a greater sense of empathy."

Working with Women

"I will tell you that the women that I know, many of them who are in this work are bad asses, dude. They are as hard-core as you can come. They've got these really giant hearts, but this really thick skin. Tough chicks who have as much capacity to love as they do to exhibit toughness.

"The dudes who are living that experience, they're living a hard, hard life. I always talk about zombie movies or end of the world apocalypse movies. You don't need to go watch *Mad Max* or *The Walking Dead* to see what it's like for people to live without the stuff that we all have in these, like, magic boxes that we live in, right? Who survives in that situation? Like, the toughest Rick Grimes of the world, right? There are many issues that affect people that are chronically homeless. Laziness is not one of them. It is so much work to be homeless. And so, you know, you get somebody like that, you know, a Rick Grimes type, and then you sit them down in an office with a twenty-five-year-old, you know, clinical, master's degree, social worker that's probably a younger woman. And like, that can be a really difficult dynamic for guys."

"But as you wrap around that person, give them some of that magic that we have around us of electricity and running water and, you know, a support network that cares about them, that loves them unconditionally, you start to see that stuff break down."

Being a Good Husband and Father

"I think that anybody who's a parent will tell you that it's the most important job that they have. It's the hardest job that there is. Liz (my wife) and I don't have a traditional marriage. For much of our lives, she was the primary breadwinner. She's always made more money than I did. And I think that I probably did struggle with that a little bit at points.

"We always try our hardest to have dinner together. We're not always successful. Sometimes I got to work later, or Liz has to work late. But nine out of ten days, we're having dinner together, and every day when we're getting ready to go to bed, we get the family together and we do something called "Rose Rose Thorn." And the concept here is that you reflect back on your day. What was a rose? That's like something that was really wonderful about your day. What was

a thorn? That is to say, like what was something that was not so great about your day? And then what is a bud? Meaning what is something that we can do tomorrow to be a little bit better? It's a really sincere approach to wrapping up the day."

Suffering and Stoicism

"I think a lot of people think that a stoic is somebody who's quiet and suffers silently. Now, I think that's bullshit. I think the virtue is in keeping your cool and not letting your emotions get the best of you, you know, that's kind of what stoicism looks like to me, you know? And God, you get alcohol involved, you see people's emotions get the best of them and fists start flying like that. There is no place in the home for that, really. There's no place for that anywhere. Letting your emotions get the best of you is the least masculine thing you can do, right? So you go to a bar, you get drunk, and you beat the shit out of somebody. It's the least masculine thing you can do because you just completely let your emotions get the best of you."

CHAPTER 10

Porn is Not
an Instruction Manual
for Sex

So much of what we've examined in this book about dudes comes down to one thing: how we relate to women. And let's be real fucking honest here, much of it breaks down to one question. Are we having sex with them?

It's tough. More women are getting degrees and want educated guys they can relate to, but we aren't going to college as much. Young women are defining success more in terms of their careers and mental health, while most younger guys still rate a family and a house as their biggest goals.

Dating apps and their algorithms make it even more frustrating. It takes 200 swipes for the average guy to get a coffee date. Once we do go out, a lot of us wonder what the rules are now. It's new. It's complicated. It can be super frustrating.

Manosphere influencers get a lot of attention by trying to make it simpler. People like Pete Hegseth, Ben Shapiro, and Jesse Watters want us to think of all women as baby-makers and raisers, taking away their identity as complete people with all that "submit to your husband" bullshit.

Meanwhile, the Andrew Tates of the world just see women as sex objects, worth nothing more than their bodies.

This really pisses me off. Screw these guys. We don't need to cede the field to them. Let's take the bull by the horns and regain the advantage for the good guys.

To do that, we need to talk about sex.

Men are Scared to Talk Sex

I love the *Dan Le Batard Show*. For years on ESPN Radio, these goofy, eccentric fellas from Miami would talk about sports, but weren't afraid to make fun of people who take them too seriously. When they moved to podcasts, their lunacy helped me get through COVID when I was commuting to the toughest job I ever had...more on that later.

The few times they talk about sex, though, it gets weird.

In 2024, there was this quote by Executive Producer Mike Ryan Ruiz. "I win in the margins. I'm basically Scott Hattaberg for fucking. Lotta walks, but I'm on base. Other dudes, they can be Giambi. I know my role." If you've seen the Brad Pitt movie *Moneyball*, you get this. Giambi hit a ton of home runs.

Former NFL defensive back and current ESPN analyst Dominique Foxworth substitutes as a host once in a while. He heard the above conversation and wanted them, and all of us frankly, to be more like Giambi. So the next time he was in charge, he brought on sex expert April Lampert to talk about how to improve lovemaking. When she brought up the clitoris, the embarrassed laughter and discomfort in the room was overwhelming.

In August of 2024, there was a discussion about what

kind of movies they would be embarrassed to watch on a public plane. The topic led to whether violence or nudity was more embarrassing, especially with children around. Affable producer Chris Cote said, "I would rather a kid see murder than boobs." He was talking about how easy it is to tell a kid that murder isn't real, but he made an unbelievably accurate point without even realizing it:

American guys are so bothered by sex, we'd rather our kids see violence than boobs.

Newspaper stories, academic studies, documentaries, and books have been written about how the Motion Picture Association of America does its movie ratings. This is the G, PG, PG13, and R system we all know about. They all came up with the same conclusion: American audiences are far more squeamish about sex than violence, and the ratings system reflects that. You're more likely to get an R rating for a movie with a sex scene than one where John Wick is mowing through enemies with a pencil.

Ask yourselves, gentlemen, are you more comfortable with gunfights, broken bones, and bloody sidewalks than conversations about sex? If so, you are not alone. But I would also ask why? What about it makes us so awkward?

Is it because we worry we won't be good at it? Maybe we are scared a woman will reject us after? Do we think God won't like it, or that talking about our bodes when other men around "makes us gay?"

It's an important conversation that we should really be honest about, though, with ourselves and our partners. We can't talk about sex in the 2020's, though, without talking about porn.

Porn is Not an Instruction Manual!

When did you first see porn? If you are a bit younger and reading this, let me be the old man and tell you something... you used to have to work for it.

My first time was in middle school back in the '80s, some kid in the neighborhood stole one of his old man's *Penthouse* mags. He wrapped it in plastic and hid it in a tree stump on these trails we used to ride our bikes on. Word got around and a few of us would ride back and look at it once in a while. I'd never seen anything like it.

It sure wasn't the last time, though. With everyone online now, it's not just easy to get porn. It's shoved at you. 93% of boys report having been exposed to porn before the age of eighteen.

This is a huge problem for a ton of reasons. Porn use is addictive, keeps you inside and lonely, hurts men's relationships, makes it harder for you to get hard, and creates unrealistic expectations.

I'm not saying don't ever watch it. But I ask that you please not think of it as a user's guide. Why?

Because it's fake.

Dick Size

Ask most women, and they will tell you something you may have trouble believing; you do not need a massive penis to satisfy her. 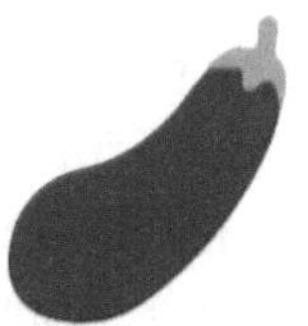

I get it. Many of us secretly think they are lying and just saying that because they want us to feel better. More men want a bigger dick than want to be taller. But why do we not trust the women who are straight up with us? Is it because we've seen porn? If the answer deep down is yes, let's have a real honest conversation about what porn is.

The average size women prefer for one time sex is 6.4 inches, erect. For long-term relationships they want something slightly smaller at 6.3 inches. No, that is not a lie. There is actually research on this shit. The average erect penis is around 5.2 inches, which is a little smaller than what women might prefer, but not by much. Are there a few women out there, "size queens," who like a bigger than average dick? Yes. But for every one of them, there are ten whose reaction is "get that thing away from me."

Porn directors, though, aren't making films for women. They look for guys with bigger dicks, usually between 7-7.5 inches. Director Adam Glasser has worked on hundreds of films so he knows what he is talking about. He explains the situation:

"There are only a certain percentage of women who can actually handle and enjoy an abnormally large bratwurst. I encounter situations like this constantly when I'm filming, and I see the signs when I watch other adult movies.

"There's the obvious grimace of pain on the actress' face—because he's way too big for her and it hurts—or the less obvious woman's hand on the man's hip to prevent him from penetrating too deep.

"I usually edit out these 'pain indicators' because, at least for me, it's distracting. It takes away from the fantasy and just reminds you that these are actors doing a job—and sometimes that job can be a pain in the ass...or vagina."

If you don't trust a dude telling you this, fair enough. But I ask you to listen to Kayden Kross. She's in not one but two porn halls of fame and has had in-depth discussions about penis size. She says that porn is all about camera angles, and bigger sizes are needed to get the right shot. It has nothing to do with the pleasure of the woman. Another legend, Nina Hartley, who started doing films in the early '80s and is still working, says that a huge dick every night is actually uncomfortable. She goes on, "Guys don't need a big cock. They need cock control. They need to last for a solid thirty minutes."

If you are asking yourself why this is case, it's an excellent question. The answer is pure biology. When aroused, vaginas expand. But unstimulated, the average depth is about three inches. Without proper foreplay or lube, just sticking it in can hurt. If you're too big, it will hurt more. Plus, some women get super uncomfortable when you hit their cervix. It's at the top of the vagina and not designed for impact. Can it feel good for certain women AFTER a proper warm up? Yes. But not all the time. This is why the actresses who Butts mentions push back when a male actor goes too deep.

Another hard fact? Only 20% of women report orgasms just from penetration. Most women orgasm from stimulating the clitoris, the small, round part at the top of her vulva. It is the only piece of the human body, on either a man or a woman, that evolved solely for pleasure. Since it extends outside of her body, you don't need to be a foot-long to do the right thing there. It's a great place to use your mouth or fingers.

Timing

Glasser, the director, describes what the timing is like to put together a fifteen to twenty minutes scene.

"We have become accustomed to watching porn studs pound away at their costars for anywhere from twenty to sixty minutes. What you don't see is what happens before the cameras start rolling—like the pill-popping and penis-injecting. In my experience, 95 percent of the male performers use some sort of erectile-enhancement medication, and the ones who don't are at the bottom of the totem pole.

"You only see the finished product, so you don't see all the stopping and starting that happens during a shoot. There are breaks to eat and drink, or catch their breath, or regain an erection, which could also mean popping another pill or sticking another needle into the base of the performer's penis. There are bathroom breaks and re-lubing breaks and still-picture-taking breaks. It's endless.

"Truth be told, neither the male or female performers are actually going at it nonstop for anywhere near the periods of time that it seems."

Again, what they are giving you is illusion made for cameras. It's not real.

Foreplay

Sex is more than just penetration. You may know this already, but the stuff you do that is not putting your dick in her is called foreplay. Kissing, touching each other with your hands, oral sex, hell, even dirty talk...all of it can be super fun. Women need to get their blood flowing to get wet, and the more stimulation you have before going in, the better this gets. If it doesn't hurt, she can enjoy it more AND it can do wonders for getting you hard as well.

Ask many women, and they will also probably tell you

this: foreplay doesn't have to just be a physical thing. A quick text asking how her day was, telling her how great she looks, or just spending quality time with her can make things better in bed. Sean Connery's character in the movie *Finding Forrester* may have said it best, "The key to a woman's heart is an unexpected gift at an unexpected time."

If this is true, you may ask yourself why most foreplay doesn't appear in porn either? And that would be another excellent question. As Glasser talks about, most videos are made to be visually appealing to men...so there is a lot less attention paid to women. The only concession you get is *sometimes* the dude goes down on a woman for a minute or two, but most of the time she sucks him off or uses her hands just to get ready for straight fucking.

There is research on this too. Less than 2% of porn for straight people has any kissing, caressing, or sweet-talking at all. 50% to 90% of videos show the woman going down on the guy, but less than 20% show a dude eating out a female partner.

So guys, when you get with a woman, it might be good to remember that most of the time, she probably doesn't want you going straight in there like you see on Pornhub. If you take some time for both of you to explore, the experience will most likely be better for both of you.

Communication/Connection

This might be the most important thing we talk about in terms of porn sex vs the real thing. In straight, guy-on-girl porn, there is almost never conversation. Less than 27% of videos have any verbal communication at all. Sweet talk, questions, or statements of what feels good are rare. And almost half of any communication is aggressive words by the dude.

Think about the last videos you watched. Did it have a blowjob or hand job, followed by some dude pounding away until he cums? The answer is probably yes. But I ask you to think about this. Is every woman the same? No. So maybe use exploration, finding out what works for her and showing her what works for you, as part of the fun? Does she like it fast or slow? Do you? Do certain parts of her body respond more to your touch than others? Does a thing she is doing really get you doing?

And while guys tend to focus on finishing, do you also want to give her pleasure? If so, it might be good to remember that many women report sex can be fun without an orgasm every time. Other factors like stress, hydration, mood, and whether she feels safe can all affect her experience. We are not machines, and that is OK.

The best way to figure this stuff out? Two things. First, you can ask her. When a woman feels comfortable, she can be more open to exploring and initiating. And let's be really clear, while many experts want you asking questions all the time, like "Can I put my hand here?", constantly doing so while you are both hot and heavy can get annoying. This is the opinion of more than a few women I know. To make that less of an ordeal, try talking to her beforehand about what works for her, what works for you, and what you both don't like.

Also, if you don't get a chance to talk beforehand, pay attention to her when she communicates with you non-verbally. If she's moaning, or grabs you tighter, or her legs start shaking, those are signs that you should probably keep going with whatever you are doing. If she is tensing up, or pulling back, those are ways of her saying she might be uncomfortable and wants something different. Respect that shit, and change gears.

Maybe think about talking to her after as well? She might tell you how much she liked something, but don't take it personally if something wasn't good. If she trusts you enough to let you know what she wants next time, that means there might actually be a next time. Plus, if she is sharing, that is an opportunity for you as well. Telling her what you liked, and asking if she would like to try other things that turn you on, is a way to expand your world.

The other thing communicating with a woman can do that most porn doesn't care about? It creates connection. Many women get more out of sex when they can be emotionally close to you. If she can feel close, intimate, and establish trust with you, she is more likely to enjoy the experience and share that joy with you. Which, again, makes the whole thing way better for everyone.

Some free advice? Talking includes remembering her name. You almost never see this in porn. Forgetting is a huge self-own.

Communicating will make you a better lover, man. Seriously. Embrace it.

Now that we've got the porn mythology out of the way, we'll spend the next chapter on other important issues: consent, protection, and pregnancy.

◆

CHAPTER 11

Consent, Pregnancy, and STIs.

When I was a State Representative in 2017, I witnessed a sexual assault without knowing it. Ironically, it was after a fundraiser for EMERGE, the group supporting female Democrats.

As I was walking back to my car after the event, I saw a man and a woman who looked to be holding each other. I couldn't see their faces in the dark, but recognized the dude as a State Senator from his distinctive and annoying voice as he loudly asked her to kiss him. I knew he was married and that wasn't his wife, but figured it wasn't my business so didn't butt in.

I got a text the next morning from the woman, a lobbyist for various causes, asking if I saw the interaction. I told her yes, and what I learned next still pisses me off. She told me the whole thing wasn't consensual, that he wouldn't let her go, and she was scared shitless because she couldn't get away.

I told her I would back her up if she wanted to report it. She didn't at the time, but a few years later when other women came forward about this guy, she decided to. So, I testified to the attorney doing the official investigation—and he concluded that yeah, the dude did this a lot.

Prick.

So many ladies are terrified of straight guys with good reason. One in five American women say they were either raped or someone tried to rape them in their lifetimes. 81% report that they experienced some form of sexual harassment or assault.

A female friend told me recently that, on the first day of a new job, the dude that hired her asked her to stand up in a group meeting and turn around to show everyone "what his wife should be jealous of."

The President of the United States bragged about being able to grab women by the pussy, was found by a court to have assaulted women, and was elected again.

The result of all this? 62% of women report today that they find men their age "frightening." Interestingly, 41% of dudes agreed. Probably the most glaring, real-life example of this is the "Man or Bear" debate. A TikTok video in 2024 asked a question to seven women: would you rather be alone in the woods with a man or a bear? Six of them chose the bear. The video went viral, with sixteen million views in two months. Most women said the bear was more predictable, treated women as humans, and wouldn't murder or rape them.

Consent

Gentlemen, this might sound preachy, and for that I am sorry. But it really is up to us to get better. Most of the time we are going to be the bigger, stronger person in a couple. If we want any kind of physical relationship with a woman, from a one-night stand to a long-term marriage, we need to man up and get better in regards to consent.

Consent is an agreement that has to be mutually accepted between people to engage in anything sexual. In real terms, both of you have to be cool with whatever you're doing. It also means a few more things.

Former Giants Linebacker Lawrence Taylor, whom Donald Trump likes to hold up as a role model for young men, is a convicted sex offender. He had sex with a sixteen-year-old when he was fifty-two. This is called "statutory rape" because consent means that whoever you are with has to *be old enough*, legally and with enough life experience, to agree to sex. If not, it's rape.

Remember when Andrew Tate told dudes the way to have a threesome is to find two women, give them "martinis, martinis, martinis, martinis," and then "bang, threesome"? This is fucked up. If you have sex with a girl who is not *sober and alert*, it's not consensual and it makes you a rapist.

Harvey Weinstein, a famous film producer, is now in prison for rape. For years, he would hold "auditions" for women who wanted to get into his movies. If you wanted in, you had to put out. But now he's in jail because consent means you can't be *coerced or threatened* into sex. Otherwise, you are a rapist.

So how do you approach this?

First, don't be an *asshole*. If you are thirty, and she looks sixteen, don't go there. If she is obviously drunk, don't go there. If you're a manager, don't dangle a job to a woman in exchange for a blowjob.

Second, ask. Like we talked about in the last chapter, a lot of women don't want you to ask, "Is this OK?" for everything, all the time, in bed. However, you can ask if you can kiss her on a first date without it being a turn-off, and go from there. And if she ever tells you "no," "stop," "I don't want that," "um-mmmmm," or anything close to those things, you need to *stop immediately*.

Third, it is so important to pay attention to her non-verbal cues. If she pushes you away, refuses to make eye contact, shakes her head, or just lays there without moving, you should *stop and ask if she is OK*.

Fourth, she has the right *to change her mind*. She may have said yes five years or five minutes ago. That doesn't mean she can't want something else now. Be OK with that.

Fifth, all this stuff *applies to you* too. 1 in 6 men and boys have reported being the victim of sexual assault. And almost 2 million American men have reported being stalked. Men make up 75% of lifetime penetrative rapists against other men. For other forms of assault with male victims, almost two-thirds of perpetrators are female.

It's not OK if someone does something to you without your agreement. Consent is a two-way street.

Pregnancy and Protection

Sex can be amazing, and contrary to some religious folks' teaching, it's not just to have kids. It feels wonderful, is great for your mental and physical health, and good sex can bring couples closer emotionally.

But if you engage in it, you need to ask yourself a couple of questions. Do I want kids? Do I want them right now? Because sex IS where babies come from. And unfortunately, there are some myths that we might need to break if you have gotten some bad information.

When I was in high school, teen pregnancy was on the rise around the country. I remember talking to a teacher over at my sister's middle school where a thirteen-year-old got pregnant. Apparently, the dude told her she couldn't get pregnant if they did it while she was standing up.

Wrong.

Here are some other myths:

- *"She can't get pregnant the first time you have sex."*
  Dude, she can.
- *"You're safe if you do it in water."*
  You're not.
- *"Pulling out always works."*
  It doesn't. Timing is hard, and there is sperm in your pre-cum.
- *"She won't get pregnant if the penis doesn't go all the way in."*
  False.
- *"She can't get pregnant during her period."*
  Your sperm can live for five days, so...Nah.
- *"Teens can't get pregnant."*
  If she's had her period, she can.

There is a simple solution to this. Use a condom. They are really effective at preventing pregnancy. Sure, they don't feel as good as bare skin, but is that sensation really worth having to deal with a pregnancy you don't want or aren't ready for?

There are other types of birth control a woman can take; a daily pill, a ring in her vagina, an implant in her arm, or semi-annual shots. These work really well, but they don't stop STIs and aren't something you control.

A Sexually Transmitted Infection (STI) is not fun. Some, that you have probably heard of, are mild and easily curable with antibiotics, like gonorrhea (the clap) and chlamydia. Others are also mild but you're stuck with them for the rest of your life, like herpes. There are lesser known ones as well, like mycoplasma genitallium, which is nasty and may take multiple doses of antibiotics to beat.

Some will kill your ass. Syphilis is curable with an antibiotic shot, but if you don't get one, it will eventually make you crazy and then take you out. HIV is also with you for the rest of your life. Drugs have turned it into something you can live with (see Magic Johnson). But if you don't take them, it will likely turn into AIDS and your immune system will go to shit. A virus that you would normally just deal with, like the flu, will then put you down.

Look, if you have sex, getting an STI is always a risk. But condoms are a safe, easy, and cheap way to reduce your risk. Some ladies are allergic to latex ones, so maybe think about Trojan, Durex, and Skyn non-latex versions.

Also, if you are going at it with multiple women at the same time, get tested regularly even if you feel fine. It can take a while for STI symptoms to show up—and sometimes, you'll never experience symptoms. But if you've got it, you can still pass it along.

If you are getting around, that's OK as long as you're honest with your partners and get tested. A lot of city or state health offices offer free testing for HIV, syphilis, gonorrhea, and chlamydia. It doesn't take long, and it will give you the information to play around without passing along bad shit.

If you either don't want kids or have had some and don't want any more, consider a vasectomy. This is where a specialty doctor, called a urologist, snips the tube allowing your sperm to get into your semen. It makes sure your swimmers don't get out when you cum.

I got mine in 2022 after the Supreme Court allowed states to make abortion illegal in places like Texas, where I was living at the time. It seems like birth control is always on the woman in our society, which isn't fair because it takes two to tango. So I went and got the snip. I was even in a story in *Business Insider* about it.

It's quick, easy, and simple. You'll be out of there in twenty minutes. However, you will have swollen balls for a few weeks, and the first few days are the worst. It's best to get it done on a day when you can take some time off to rest after. A ton of dudes do it the morning of the first Thursday of March Madness and watch ball all weekend. Make sure you have ice packs or frozen peas around to help with the swelling. Don't work out or do anything to put pressure on your boys for a couple of weeks, like squats, riding a bike, or jumping up and down at a sporting event.

Trust me, less than two weeks after mine, I couldn't help myself when MLS team Austin FC won a playoff game on penalty kicks and I went crazy. Ten minutes later, I realized the mistake and I immediately had to waddle home and go for the ice.

Don't Be a Dick

The name of this project is *Being a Man in the 21st Century Without Being a Dick*. Nowhere is this more of a thing than when it comes to sex. So:

- Make sure you never, ever use your physical strength, booze, drugs, or professional power to get a woman in bed when she doesn't want to. This is basic.
- Understand that pregnancy is SO MUCH more of a risk to a woman than you, especially if you're in a state where abortion is illegal. Respect that fact and her by taking control over what you can with condoms...or even better, if you never want kids, a vasectomy.
- Get tested if you are getting around.

This stuff can be uncomfortable. I get it. But men take responsibility for their actions, and that means taking on hard issues head-on.

CHAPTER 12

Young Men aren't Approaching Women

On a recent episode of the *Daily Show*, comedian Leslie Jones went off on men. Though her yelling style works as a funny strategy for that audience, and especially the women watching who agree with her, it's not going to effectively reach many who need help.

That being said, her content isn't wrong. From men not washing their own assholes because they worry about being gay, to guys not having role models and being unwilling to get therapy, her critiques are real and something we should listen to.

One point in particular she mentioned stuck out to me... nearly 50% of single young men report not having approached a woman in the past year. Nearly three in four young women report wanting to be talked to more by guys, but we just aren't doing it.

There are two big reasons for this.

No Reps

The growth of social media and other types of virtual communication sure is one of the reasons. In 2003, young people reported to the U.S. Bureau of Labor Statistics Time Use Survey that they socialized in person sixty-one minutes per day. By 2019, that number dropped thirty-nine minutes per day. Why?

The first big social media platform was actually MySpace, which started in 2003. YouTube was founded in 2005 and both Facebook and Twitter became open to the general public in 2006. Since then, short video apps like Tiktok and Instagram have become widely used, and streaming services like Twitch help keep gamers on their screens. This year, 80% of 18-29 year-olds report using Instagram, with half of them saying they go on Tiktok at least once per day.

So as the easy and addictive nature of social media communication became popular, the practice of actually meeting people in person started dropping.

COVID made things worse. While older people cut social time the most during COVID, they at least bounced back a little after lockdowns ended. Young people continued the trend of not talking to each other in person, and have never recovered. It's almost like they forgot how to do it.

Anything in life that you want to be good at requires practice. It's why athletes repeat the same movements over and over, or why scholars spend years in study. The more you do something, the more reps you get in, the better you are at it.

So one of the reasons dudes aren't approaching women? They aren't getting their social reps in, and they're out of practice. But, there's another big reason.

"Being Labeled a Creep, Going Viral for a Simple Convo"

The same research that found young men aren't approaching women found that over 70% of young women say that they want to be approached more. The issue is that guys get conflicting messages from online conversations and media.

Stories about dating on Tiktok are dominated by women, and most of them revolve around risks, harassment, and deception. The "Man vs Bear" debate described earlier is a great example. Posts with the #97percent hashtag, focusing on a report that 97% of women had received some kind of sexual harassment, got over 300 million views. This message that men should stay away from women is also backed up in popular media. Sabrina Carpenter's song, "Manchild," debuted at #1 on Billboard's Top 100 last year, and includes lyrics telling men she doesn't want them approaching her and just to let her be. For the people from my generation, think TLC's "No Scrubs" as a comparison.

Meanwhile, the smaller number of men talking about this topic online report being rebuffed by women when they approach on the street, at the bookstore, in the gym, or at the club. And many guys, after the #MeToo movement, don't want to come across as jerks. 44% of young men say that fear of being labeled as creepy makes them less likely to initiate in-person contact with a women.

So they go to dating apps, which have their own issues.

Most are sausage fests. Bumble has the most equity of users with 54% of accounts being men. Hinge has a 60%-40% male to female ratio, and Tinder has 67% of its accounts being dudes. On Tinder, the average guy gets about 5 matches for every 100 swipes. An average woman gets 44. So, while woman may have some valid complaints about the type of men they are matching with, they get more attention, more conversations, and more real-life meat-ups off the apps than men.

Why does this hurt so bad for guys who want relationships? Apps are now where marriages come from. In 2025 over 50% of engaged couples, and 27% who actually tied the knot, met on one of them.

So, the frustration and anger that builds up from being rejected over and over again can take a toll. And that leads to just withdrawing from making any attempts.

Women Have a Point

However, there are two sides to every story. To the fellas out there reading this, women have their own mixed feelings about interacting with us. "Me Too," the movement that led so many men to not want to be viewed as creeps, happened for a reason.

Women describe men as their "alpha predator," and numbers back this up.

- 1 in 5 American women has either been raped or someone has tried to rape her. That's a lot of women.
- Nearly 4 in 10 workers report witnessing sexual harassment at work, and women report experiencing harassment firsthand more than men.
- A majority of young women (aged 18-34) has received a dick pic from guys...and most of those are ones they didn't ask for.

This is some serious shit, and almost every woman you meet will have a horror story about an experience with a man. Some of them will be really, really bad. You need to respect that fact and keep it in mind when you talk to her.

And if she doesn't want to talk to you at that moment, don't take it personally. Life is tough for all of us right now in a number of ways, and her reluctance may actually have nothing to do with you.

So What To Do?

This is a hard nut to crack. So fellas, if we are interested in meeting women in real life, what can we do?

- The easiest thing? Don't be an asshole. Women don't like it when you are mean, or when you send dick pics without consent, so don't do that.
- When you do approach a woman, try talking to her about something that isn't threatening or overtly sexual. As an example, if she is wearing a shirt of a band you like, maybe compliment her on that and ask whether or not she's seen them lately.
- If you want to help a woman, ask first. Let's say you pick up her bags at the airport without asking her… that can be creepy. So just asking, "Would you like help with that?" allows you to be polite and helpful without seeming like you think she cannot handle it herself.
- LISTEN. We dudes, and yes that includes yours truly, can sometimes get in a conversation and make it all about ourselves. We try to impress by showing our

expertise, or talk all about our own lives. Many women like these discussions to be two-way streets. So ask genuine questions, and show genuine interest... even if you know the answer, let her get her points out. Channel your inner Ted Lasso and "Be curious, not judgmental."

- You can also show some emotion, connecting with a woman, without getting too heavy. Be honest and genuine, but saying things like, "I had a tough childhood," can be seen as trying to be manipulative. That can come later after you get to know her.

- If you want to keep talking, instead of asking for her number right away, maybe ask her for coffee at a public place at an agreed upon time. Or offer her your phone number so she doesn't feel threatened.

- ACTUALLY MEET IN REAL LIFE. So many guys, because they are stressed about it not working, will text constantly instead of committing to a real meet. So, set a time and place...and then show up.

For your online profiles, try actually writing something out. Just putting a picture of yourself out there with the line "HMU" (Hit Me Up) doesn't show women any kind of depth.

And for app pictures? Try taking some in different situations. I hear over and over again how just pictures with fish aren't the best way to introduce yourself, and bathroom selfies are apparently not great either. If you have a female friend, maybe ask her help in terms of what women might be looking for as well.

At the end of the day, gentlemen, relationships with women are good for us. To get them, we have to reach out and say hi. So let's put the reps in, and get better with this stuff.

CHAPTER 13

Healthier, Happier...
and Not Scared
to Have a Girl Over

Author's Note: *This chapter was requested by SO many women. It might seem simplistic, but their experiences in single guys' places is something talked about pretty commonly. This is true even for older men. If you live with a partner in a clean, well-apportioned place, you can probably skip this one. If not, read on.*

Single men, this one is directly for you.

I was lucky enough to take a woman back to my place one time. After a thoroughly enjoyable evening, on the way out, she thanked me for having clean sheets. My reply was a little shocked. "Yeah? I mean, you're welcome, but isn't that a given?"

Her reply was immediate. "Oh god no. You would be surprised."

As I have relayed that story to various women I know, they regale me with stories about dudes' places.

"He had hair on his bar of soap in the shower."

"I recently heard a story from a friend who is 'trying' to date men. She went over to a man's house and asked if she could have some water. The man then proceeded to walk to the fridge, grab the remnants of a takeout cup of soda, dumped it out, rinsed the cup, and then filled it with water for her."

"One of my friends once told me how when she asked for a glass of water, she was given tap water in a bowl, like a cat."

"In his bedroom was just a bed. Had a bed frame but nothing else. Not one other thing. I don't need some cluttered place with lots of decor, but he literally owned three pieces of furniture."

"I once visited an apartment of this Army buddy and his roommate. They had a mountain of beer cans neatly arranged and still building."

"He had a milk crate for a nightstand."

"His bedroom had no bedframe. Only an inflatable mattress."

"One of my college boyfriends would let his toilet build up black scum. Ugh, that was so embarrassing for me."

Internet memes about how guys only have a mattress, computer, TV, and weight set with captions like "Men really think its OK to live like this" have hundreds of thousands of likes and shares from women on social media. One even says, "When you're at his place; +1 for if he has a bathroom trash can, +2 if he has hand towels, +3 throw pillows, +2 separate bottle of body wash, shampoo & conditioner, +2 bed frame, +2 any fresh produce, +1 clean sheets, +1 night stand. If he has more than 8 points, you can sleep with him."

Men, come on now. We need to get better at this shit. Basic hygiene in the place we live is a way for us to be more upstanding, responsible people. If you have a clean house that you are proud to live, work, and play in, you are going to feel better about yourself, have a more positive outlook on life, and make it less likely you will get sick.

A place you aren't proud of, though, has the opposite effect. It contributes to stress and depression. It can make you sick and worsen allergies. And, as we've seen from above, if you do ever get a woman over, the experience will stick with her. She probably won't want to come back and will leave feeling even more frustrated that men do not seem capable of basic life skills.

Then you'll end up in one of these stories.

Dude. Don't be that guy.

This isn't all about women we want to date. So many of us are bunkering down, not socializing with real people in favor of online chats, games, videos, and even AI girlfriends. For our mental health to get better, we have to find ways of talking to real people and the spaces we have to meet them matter. One of these places could be your home or apartment.

No one is saying you have to live in a spotless laboratory, or spend a ton of money on leather furniture and silk sheets (especially in this economy). But there are some easy, simple things you can do to improve your place.

Basic Cleanliness

The top thing I hear from women repeatedly is complaints about the bathroom. A dirty sink, toilet, and shower is a major turn off for them. The humidity encourages bacteria, viruses, and mold growth and can make you sick.

Take some time once a week and get to cleaning. Use some paper towels for a first go, as they are going to be better at picking up things like hair and dirt. Or if you are going to use a sponge, make sure and replace it once in a while. If you use the same one over and over, all of those gross things are going to build up on it and you won't get things clean.

Get yourself a toilet brush. Use it regularly, and make sure the toilet seat is clean. Not everyone stands to pee. Clean the floor sometimes as well, and don't forget the mirror. There's no reason to let all of your toothpaste build up. If you have a shower liner, put it in a washing machine once in a while. And make sure you have a trash can that you empty regularly.

The kitchen is another area where water and food can build up and create problems. Wash your dishes regularly, take out the trash and recycling when the cans are full, and if you use your stove or microwave make sure to clean those things once in a while.

Don't leave food in the refrigerator too long. New life-forms growing on that Chinese takeout you had six months ago lead to bad horror movie plots.

As for the rest of the house, dusting furniture and vacuuming the floors is important. Doing laundry every week makes sure that smells don't build up and ensures you have clean clothes when going out. Also, clean sheets, as I found out directly, are a close second to bathrooms as a thing women mention as essential to a good experience.

Cleaning supplies are NOT expensive. You can find cleaner, sponges, paper towels and rags in local dollar stores for a minimal spend.

As for time, regular cleaning doesn't take a ton. I like to clean on a Saturday or Sunday during a football game. When commercials come on, I go clean for a few minutes and then come back to watch the next drive. It's also an excuse to put your phone down once in a while and do something productive you can be proud of.

Cleaning also keeps your place from getting musty and smelly, another common complaint from the ladies.

House Stuff

Fellas, basic furniture is pretty cheap. So are towels, lamps, and non-plastic plates, cups, and utensils. Again, no one is saying you have to spend a million dollars on stuff. But you can make a trip to your local thrift store, yard sales, or discount store like Ross or Marshalls to find deals on simple things.

If you have a Habitat for Humanity Re-Store in your town, those are great places for decent household items that won't destroy your bank account. They sell quality used stuff, and then use the money made to help build homes for people that need them.

In your bedroom, new bedframes for a full-sized mattress cost as little as $100. An end table, reading light, dresser, and a place to hang up some of your nicer clothes are all really easy to figure out. Make sure to use those dressers and hangers. There's no reason to have clothes thrown all over the place.

For your kitchen, get a few sets of plates, cups, and silverware. Also, some enclosed Tupperware. Even if you get delivery a lot, eating with real stuff makes for a better atmosphere. It's also better for the environment, cleaner when you wash them properly, and makes for a MUCH better experience when you have someone over.

Also, find a real table. Even a small one. And some chairs.

Make sure you always have some water available for guests. Canned fizzy water or even a clean glass for some ice and tap water (unlike the bowl example from above) if your sink water is good.

Lastly for the basics? Towels and soap. Have a clean hand towel or two for your bathroom along with some hand soap. Again, this stuff is really cheap to find and great to have for guests.

Next Level

If you can get all of this done, great! Just having a clean place with a setup where you can be proud to have people over will make you healthier, happier, and more confident. But here are a couple of more suggestions to think about.

A first aid kit. Having some supplies in case someone has a cut or splinter is always a good thing.

Get a bookcase, with some books that you actually will read!

Some pictures on the wall with frames. You don't have to go crazy, but some color on bare walls helps put everyone in a better mood.

A rug or two if you have tile floors can help make a place look homier.

A small machine with some ground coffee can come in handy.

Since keeping a clean place is SO important for your mental health, that's what we are going to be diving into in the next chapter.

CHAPTER 14

Mental Health

Author's Note: *This Chapter deals with mental health and suicidal thoughts. If you have any issues, you can get help. Just dial 988 on your phone. Calls are free, private, and available in both English and Spanish.*

The mouth of the shotgun felt pretty comfortable under my chin, and I put my hand down near the trigger to see if it would reach. It did.

I'd just gone online and looked up the best ways to kill yourself, and found a site that went over the options. It said most methods (pills, knives, hanging, etc.) didn't work very well, and were mostly about calling for help. If you didn't want to fuck around, a shotgun with buckshot or a slug fired under your chin and aimed at the brainstem was as close to certain as you were going to get.

It was January 2021. COVID had hit New Mexico the previous March, and my job at the time was Secretary of Workforce Solutions (the state's name for the Labor Department). That March, I felt like I was just hitting my stride. The Department had a hard-working and profession-al staff making for a great team. I was getting into a groove with the Governor on what she was looking for. We were starting a new Apprenticeship initiative and my baby, a new statewide STEM championship for high school students, was giving a ton of kids motivation for a bright future.

Then, COVID.

My department was in charge of the state unemploy-ment insurance program. Congress decided that, except for "essential workers," most people should stay home to stop the spread of the virus and save people's lives. In order to do that, and still pay rent and get groceries, they wanted people to apply for unemployment and use that as a vehicle for federal aid.

It was a shit show.

The unemployment system was designed in the 1930s for an economy that doesn't exist today. Huge criminal op-erations across the globe committed identity theft to fake applications, and then they'd steal taxpayer money that so many real people desperately needed. Congress and Trump only set up COVID relief systems a few months at a time, so benefits and eligibility times changed constantly.

Then there was volume. On March 10th, 2020, there were about 9,800 people in the New Mexico system. By the end of June, there were over 150,000. Everyone at the department was going flat out, but it never seemed to be enough. Though we were at the 90% level of getting help out within three weeks, a good mark, that still left SO many struggling. We hired and trained as many new people as possible, and tried to get good online systems, but people wanted SOMEONE to talk to. They were home all day, with nothing else to do, scared out of their minds, and desperate for help.

So they called. And called. And called. Everyone they knew. Every office they could think of. Over, and over, and over again. One day, we recorded 637,000 calls.

New Mexico is a small state, so there are only about three degrees of separation between literally anyone. I helped a couple of folks navigate the system that first March, and they passed on my email to friends of theirs. Then, when I was able to help them, those folks passed my address on. It got out of control.

In a month, I was getting 300-400 emails every Monday, with probably 1,000 more scattered throughout the week. Every week. For over a year. And I heard all the stories.

"Please, I need help. I don't know how much longer I can keep my kids."

"I had to start living in my car. Please help. I am desperate."

"Just wanted to let you know, my neighbor tried to kill herself because she couldn't get help the other day."

I personally helped at least 10,000 people that year, and they kept coming back for more. I barely slept. In April of 2020, I passed out on the floor of my office, then had a panic attack so bad, my deputy had to call an ambulance because of the hyperventilation. Someone fire bombed a state car in one of our parking lots right after Thanksgiving. People with my position in different states had police escorts because of death threats. I was so miserable, I left my relationship of seven years in December. I just couldn't do it. The only emotions I felt were a bleak, numb emptiness with spikes of pure, concentrated rage.

All of that led to the night with the shotgun. I didn't end up pulling the trigger. I thought about my mom, and wondered who would take care of my dog Cooper. Plus, I remembered I only had bird shot shells and that probably wasn't going to do the trick. Rather than going and buying some buckshot, though, I did call my boss in the governor's office the next day. I told her I almost painted my wall with my brains the night before, and said I was probably done. Her reply probably saved my life.

"Can I try and find you some help?"

I said yes.

She set up an appointment for me with a therapist who specialized in first responders: cops, frontline nurses, folks like that. He was brilliant. The guy helped me recognize that my anger was actually born from a lack of control, went through some ways to help me manage my emotions when stress got crazy, and educated me on strategies for how to not take things too personally.

And thanks to this help, and my willingness to take it, I'm still here writing this.

That story is why manosphere types who put down mental health help piss me off.

Accused rapist Andrew Tate constantly punches down at men living with depression, implying that mental health issues stem from being weak and not experiencing enough "conquest." Streamer Sneako, the winner recently ser-enaded by twelve-year-old fans with chants of "Fuck the women" and "All gays must die," once told a guy he "wasn't a real man" because he took antidepressants. Myron Gaines, from the *Fresh and Fit Podcast* and author of the book *Why Women Deserve Less*, once said depression isn't real, therapy is a scam, and anyone who claims to be sad is a loser and a fucking bitch.

Fellas, don't listen to these assholes. They're fucking wrong.

Jay Glazer is a real man. Currently the Sunday NFL reporter for Fox, he is one of the most successful examples of the kind of grind culture those manosphere influencers tell everyone about. He worked his way up from an entry level position at the NY Post to now being viewed by millions every week. He fought two professional MMA fights before becoming one of the world's first MMA reporters. Now he trains Hollywood celebrities to fight.

He is not weak.

He has depression, and has recently started talking about it. He wrote a book called *Unbreakable: How I Turned My Anxiety and Depression into Motivation and You Can Too.* He has a podcast about the issue, and is a regular on other podcasts to speak about his experience. He also talks directly to NFL players about his experience, and the importance of leaning on the people around you when you need help.

His view is simple: your brain is part of your body and you should treat it for injury just like anything else. If a fighter comes into his gym and has an issue with his knee, they have to get it looked at and treated for him to fight again.

It's not embarrassing.

You're not a lesser man for getting better.

Diego Luna is a real man. Currently a soccer striker for pro side Real Salt Lake, Luna made it to the top of the U.S. pro game the hard way. He left home at fifteen to attend various youth academies, then played minor league ball in El Paso for two years. After making it to the big leagues, he played so well he is now constantly being called up by the U.S. National Team to represent the U.S. at the international level.

He is not a loser.

He recently opened up about his mental struggles. Dealing with panic attacks (I feel you, dude), loneliness, depression, constant doomscrolling on his phone, and bottling up his emotions and problems were constant issues for him, even though he admits he had people around that would help.

After his brother finally talked him into seeing a therapist, his training improved and he scored his first top flight professional goal the very next game. Seven months later, he was the MLS Young Player of the Year. Now he represents the Stars and Stripes. Therapy, he says, made him a better person as well:

"Gradually, I became the father I wanted to be. My son, Manolo, turned two years old earlier this month, and as a dad, you can't be angry all the time. You can't lock yourself in your room all day. Your highs and lows can't be extreme. You have to be the rock for your family, and I'm finally able to show my son the patience he needs. I'm a better partner, a better son, a better friend. I'm simply a better version of myself."

Dwayne "The Rock" Johnson is a real man. You know him from his stints in the WWE and all of his blockbuster movies. What you don't know is that he worked hard for his fame. After completing four years playing football at Miami, and winning a National Championship, he tried his hand at the pro game. But no one from the NFL signed him, and he only lasted for two months in the Canadian Football League before being cut. Then, he spent a year working the minor wrestling circuits learning the trade the hard way, earning $40 a match.

He is not a fucking bitch. And I would love to see Myron Gaines call him that to his face.

The superstar now openly talks about bouts of depression: the first when he got hurt as a young college football player, the second after divorcing his first wife in 2008, and his third in 2017. He also talks about how his mom tried to kill herself in front of him. She pulled over on the highway and tried to jump in front of traffic when he was fifteen, after they got thrown out of their apartment.

By his third bout of depression, though, he knew how to reach out for help. Today, on his social media, he preaches the positive impacts of therapy and learning coping skills to others with issues. "If you're going thru your own version of mental wellness turning into mental hell-ness, the most important thing you can do is talk to somebody. It can't be fixed if you keep that pain inside. Having the courage to talk to someone is your superpower. I lost two friends to suicide."

Other examples?

- NBA Champion Kevin Love is a real man, who, after dealing with panic attacks, finally shook the "real men don't talk about their feelings" and go it alone bullshit. He got help and is still playing.

- All Pro Cowboys QB Dak Prescott is a real man. His brother died by suicide, and now he is an advocate for mental health to keep others from doing the same thing.
- Former SNL Comedian and movie star Pete Davidson is a real man who openly talks about his own struggles with mental health. He has PTSD from when he was a kid (his father was a firefighter who died in the World Trade Center on 9/11) and he is diagnosed with Borderline Personality disorder. He advocates for therapy and antidepressants.
- Seth Mouton is a real man. Now a Congressman, the Army Vet served four tours in Iraq. In office, he pushed for the VA to reduce wait time for therapy, introduced mental health screenings into regular doctor visits, and increased telehealth opportunities, including creating a national suicide hotline for vets.

The moral of the story? Don't listen to Andrew Tate. Don't listen to Sneako. Don't listen to Gaines, or anyone else selling these tired lines.

Real men step up and do the hard thing. They talk to someone and get better. Period.

Want to step up yourself? Try the following:

Talk to a professional.

If you have a regular doctor, they can help get you to one. When I was having issues in the fall of 2024, I almost beat up a guy in the middle of a street. I knew I needed to deal with this crap again and went to my doc. She said to look at *Psychology Today*, which she described as "like a dating app for therapists." Through the website, I found a great therapist, and he has helped tremendously.

If you don't have a ton of money, that's OK. Your local Federally Qualified Health Clinic (FQHC) has some great folks working there. They do mental health services and will generally charge you what you can afford.

If you prefer therapy by online chat, there are some wonderful low cost options out there like Talkspace and BetterHelp.

If you are feeling like you want to take a shotgun to your own head; don't. Instead, pick up the phone and call someone who will listen to you. Just dial 988. The talk is free, and private.

Even if you start feeling better after getting help from a pro, think about continuing it. Look at it like your car. If you take it in for regular maintenance, you are less likely to have your engine blow up on you. If you keep your brain and emotions feeling good regularly, you are less likely to need the 988 number.

Don't Sit at Home, Alone

After avoiding the street fight, the therapist I found asked how I dealt with things when I was got depressed or suicidal. I responded that I tended to just bunker down at home and binge Netflix 'til I felt better. His immediate response was "DON'T DO THAT."

See, isolation over time gets you more stressed. That is really bad for your brain and it eventually makes you more depressed.

If you are feeling bad, take a friend out for a coffee. Watch the game with some friends. Find someone, and do something. It will help, **EVEN IF YOU'RE AN INTROVERT**. I know some of us need time alone to recharge, but getting your ass out at least once in a while and interacting with others is the way to a better place.

Lay Off the Booze

I know a drink when you're feeling bad can help in the short term, or so my Irish genes tell me. But here's the problem with the booze: alcohol is a depressant, slowing down your brain activity and getting in the way of your emotional regulation.

So when your buzz wears off it can make you feel worse than when you started, and I'm not just talking about a hangover. It also makes it harder to get good sleep. And when you're tired, the body releases stress hormones that make you feel worse.

Sleep

Speaking of sleep, did you know people with insomnia are ten times more likely to have depression and seventeen times more likely to have anxiety than the general population? Sleep is what your body and brain need to recover from the day, process memories, and get reloaded for the next day. Without it, you get more stressed and are less able to fight off negative emotions. When you're depressed, you are less likely to sleep, creating a downward spiral leading to a really shitty place.

So work really hard to get that seven to eight hours a night. It will make you happier.

Ease Up on the Fast Food

This is one of the few things I agree with RFK Jr on. Fast food, with a ton of refined sugar, saturated fats, and ultra-processed ingredients lead to inflammation. That means your body treats it like an allergic reaction, releasing chemicals to fight what it sees as foreign objects. Imagine your gut reacting to a bee sting. That ain't good.

Plus, with all the sugar, the rapid rise and fall in energy levels does nothing to help stabilize your mood. So eat less McDonalds if you're feeling bad.

Do Something Physical

Go for a walk. Seriously. It gets the blood moving in your body and releases "feel good" hormones, giving you more energy and helping you sleep better. It is shown to help thinking and makes it easier to decompress from stress. And if you can get out in the sun, all the better. Being in nature has been a cure for bad moods for generations, and the sun will get your body making Vitamin D to help fight depression.

But any kind of exercise works. Lifting weights has the same kind of effect as a walk or run, and the breathing and stretching work in yoga helps your brain process stress better. Whatever your preference, get your body moving. It will help.

Pet a Dog

Or a cat. Or a horse. Petting animals is shown to reduce cortisol, the stress hormone, and release more of a bonding hormone called oxytocin. It's why therapy dogs are brought in to help people with mental health disorders and after traumatic events like school shootings.

My dog isn't trained for much and he's terrible at guarding the house. But he's furry, cute, and loves a hug. This keeps me from pulling the trigger sometimes.

PUT DOWN YOUR FUCKING PHONE!

Social media algorithms are designed to keep you looking at your screen. Constant new videos and posts, a fear of missing out on stuff others are doing, and new likes and comments on your posts release a chemical called dopamine into your head. Your brain likes this, and so it triggers you to keep doing it. That's why your apps give you notifications all the time, to keep you coming back so companies running social media can keep selling your attention to the highest bidder.

Even worse, these companies love pushing bad news because humans are much more likely to share shootings, angry political rants, and shit-talking than good news. Seeing that stuff over, and over, and over again isn't going to make you feel better.

We'll go more into this in a later chapter, but for now, please stop the doomscrolling.

And go for a walk. You'll feel better, I promise.

CHAPTER 15

Interviews with Interesting Guys
LARRY LOUICK

Larry Louick believes in protecting people. After bouncing at a student bar near Georgetown University in Washington DC, and interacting with cops during the course of the job, he put that belief to the test and joined the profession. In total he spent twenty-five years in policing, starting out working a beat in a small town, then other roles, including two years on a SWAT team before retiring as a Criminal Division Detective.

In the later part of his career, and since retiring, he's been involved in the regulatory side of the fight game. Serving as a Commissioner with the New Mexico Athletic Commission, he has a say in votes held by the Association of Boxing Commissions and Combative Sports on the unified rules of boxing and MMA. This last summer, Larry completed the course he needed to judge boxing matches. As a fun side gig, he also serves as a referee for local professional wrestling events.

A family man, Larry and his wife (both white) made the decision to adopt a mixed race and African-American daughters. He provides some great wisdom for men today gained from a lifetime of different experiences.

Being a Cop

"You know, my parents raised three kids: a social worker, a nurse, and a cop. And I think that really says a lot about, if nothing else, how I ended up in a helping profession, albeit one that's very, very traditionally male and macho oriented. But yeah, I enjoy helping and I feel like I was able to. Working patrol, mostly nights, I made between 1200 and 1300 DWI arrests and had an over 99% conviction rate. So I feel like obviously prevented a few bad things from happening.

"Then fifteen years as a detective, I worked pretty much every type of crime there is. Like everybody else at my department, I have to start off on what we call the JV squad, the paper crimes and the property crimes. But then I moved on to the homicides and the rapes and the child abuse cases. I worked child abuse cases, child sexual abuse cases, numbering well into the triple digits. Probably the most satisfying thing is when the judge reads the jury's verdict and makes the defendant stand up and face the jury. Watching somebody hear that he's been convicted of hurting children and then watching him get led away for years is probably the most satisfying thing imaginable. It was for me at least."

Confronting Hard Problems

"On a Wednesday night, a call came in on some sort of felony level domestic violence situation, which in our department requires a detective. They sent my backup because I was busy training and as is our custom, the following morning briefing you talk about your call outs from the night before. And so my colleague, who is an absolutely wonderful human being, I love to death, has been around forever, was explaining what was going on.

"He was giving the background, and I knew just based on the information I was given the night before that this was a couple where there was a man and his trans female partner. And you know, the other detective is starting to explain it. And I'm going to say it's important to say that I know this person knows better. This person is so much an ally to the extent that he actually told me he had been an attendant in a same-sex wedding. He sometimes struggles though to use the proper words, and describing the transgender woman, I don't even want to say the word that he used, but it was a very outdated term that does not address a person's gender or gender identity. It addresses something else.

"But when he said the word, the entire room full of detectives and support staff who were assigned to the detective division just absolutely burst out in uproarious laughter at the mere mention of somebody who is either sexually or gender different. And I'm just sitting there, kind of shaking my head, and I'm thinking I got to say something. I need to correct him. And I know what the reaction is going to be. And I finally said, "Number one, the term you used doesn't even address what we're talking about and it's very outdated. But when you meet somebody like that and you're dealing with somebody like that, you need to ask them what their name is and what their pronouns are." And the room that had kind of started to die down a little bit erupts again. And I knew that was going to be the reaction, but I had to do it. I know that there are other people in that room who understand what I was saying and might feel the same way, but don't speak up.

"Anybody who knows me knows I'm a very vocal person. If I'm thinking something, I'm gonna fucking tell you what it is. I don't hold back sometimes to my detriment, and sometimes it's not always the proper venue. But I felt like I needed to do it. And we have since then had other circumstances and experiences that people have been involved in, in that same division where it needed to be addressed.

"You have to let people know that they're wrong. And when I say people are wrong, I don't mean you're wrong if your faith or your particular interpretation of your particular faith teaches you that it's wrong for a person, wrong or sinful for a person to exist exactly the way their creator made them. But it's wrong to treat them differently. You have a responsibility to treat everybody with basic human dignity and respect."

Respecting Political Differences

"At the same time, these people who may not be woke and may not understand all the terminology and feelings of the, you know, the left-wing movement? Those are the people that I know for a fact have and will continue to run towards danger with me while everybody else is running away. And what are you to do? You know, what am I supposed to do when all of my fellow lefties don't work in law enforcement? They're the ones running the other way.

"I don't think there's anything inherently cowardly or, you know, about being a lefty, but those people don't go into the jobs where you do those things. And the people whose opinions and world views I don't share and sometimes loathe are the people that I can count on to keep me safe while I'm keeping everybody else safe."

More Diversity in Policing

"The problem is you have this group of people who are resistant to social change, and law enforcement officers are some of the biggest ones. If we had more people who had the opportunity to study on a college level and be around people who are different from them and to do a lot more critical thinking and to understand things, really complex issues of poverty and its relationship to crime, socioeconomic inequality and systemic racism, I think they might deliver their services better.

"The time now is perfect for people with degrees that have no directly relatable professional field and no way in hell of ever paying back their student loans. We need more of those people.

"It's convincing them that law enforcement is a very, very appropriate place to use their skills and convincing law enforcement recruiters that you actually need that guy with the gender studies degree or the sociology degree or the social work degree."

Raising a Daughter

"Well, the number one thing is I defer to my wife. She's the genius in the relationship. I definitely punched above my weight class on that one. But she is by far, and more importantly than anything else, the most amazing human being I've ever run across. Her degree is in sociology with a minor in women's studies. She has a master's in social work. She has the highest level of professional certification as a social worker can have.

"We said early on we weren't going to hit our kids. We weren't going to use corporal punishment." I said, "I'll just get up in their face and yell out." She says no, you won't because you don't want some girl growing up, getting used to a big scary man yelling in their face and then giving him a hug two seconds later. And she would get on me about my drinking for many years and she would say, "Look, you don't want your girls used to having the man in their life always have booze on his breath."

"It's modeling. It's not so much what you say, but it's what they see."

CHAPTER 16

The Algorithm

As we just talked about extensively, one of the biggest things we can do to be happier is put our phones down. But social media companies want to keep our eyeballs glued to the screen instead of in the real world. How do they do this? It really comes down to two words you may have heard of. The algorithm.

What the hell does this even mean? An algorithm in math terms is a set of numeric instructions used to perform calculations with a specific set of data. In English, you use one when you have a bunch of information and you want a specific outcome out of it.

For social media, algorithms are computer programs designed to filter what posts you see on your social feeds. Companies feed you ones they think you'll like to maximize the time you spend on their platforms. The more time you spend there, the more paid ads you'll see, generating giant profits for them.

It's all a numbers game.

Algorithms determine what you see via a combination of things:

- You may not remember now, but when you set up your X, Instagram, and Facebook accounts, you were asked what your interests were out of the gate. Those get put into your algorithm and posts with related content start showing up.
- As you end up liking things, those likes are recorded and the program learns to spit back stuff it thinks will keep you there. Netflix and Spotify, for instance, do this with shows and music.
  If you like a lot of romcoms, Netflix puts more of them in the "recommended for you" category.
  If you like a lot of '90s rap, Spotify will throw some Tupac at you during your regular playlists.
  Where you are matters, as some social media algorithms use your geography to show posts from your area to keep you interested.
- If a topic is "trending," meaning a ton of people are talking about that thing, then you are much more likely to see it on an X account.

Ever hear the term, "going viral"? A virus is a small thing (think the cold or flu) that takes over your body's cells. Once in those cells, it makes more of itself, explodes those cells, and ejects new viruses out to infect more cells. On the internet, a post replicates itself the same way using these algorithms and everyone sharing it, with one big difference. No one chooses to spread a cold. But we all choose to spread viral social media stuff.

All of it can seem pretty innocent. I mean, there is so much out there and who wants to see posts they aren't interested in? Plus, videos of baby hippos are cute and make my day better.

But there is a much darker side to all of this coming right out of Darth Vader's playbook.

Rage and Conflict

Social media LOVES anger and fighting. Tulane University recently reported that people are much more likely to interact with a political post when they are angry with it than if they agree. Nuanced, balanced takes tend to get minimal views and shares.

It's why news channels actually don't have that much news anymore. MSNBC only has about 15% of their programming as "news" or "reporting." The other 85% are opinion shows, with hosts selling angry, conflict-oriented viewpoints. Fox News is a little better, with 45% of programming as news, but the majority of time is dedicated to opinion hosts that generate conflict. Of the three major cable news channels, only CNN (with 65% of programming for news) actually has news the majority of the time.

Hot takes sell.

This isn't just about news. Look at Stephen A Smith. He's known for his debate show on ESPN, *First Take*, where he constantly tries to beat opponents with his strongest views. If you google his name, the videos that come up have descriptions like "viciously goes after," "shocking article," and "outside confrontation with Lebron." The louder, bigger, and meaner his content is, the more exposure it gets.

Other sports shows constantly focus on topics like debating Kobe Bryant's legacy, top ten NFL power rankings for the week, or possible trades for baseball teams during the winter...making you agree or disagree immediately to keep your emotions up and your eyes glued to the content.

Why does this happen? Evolution.

The animals that made it to today, including humans, lived when others didn't because of a "fight or flight" response. Basically, our brains are wired to recognize something that could be a threat and make a quick decision to run or hit back quickly, because thinking too long could get your ass killed. When we get riled up, our brains are flooded with chemicals raising our awareness, energy levels, and making us more likely to remember something. In sports, it's why you have to go to the bathroom or throw up sometimes before a big game. Your body wants to be ready to fight or run in stressful situations, and doesn't need anything in your stomach slowing you down.

The internet LIVES on the "fight" part of fight or flight. Your evolved sense of threat recognizes something that pisses you off, and keeps your attention there without you even knowing it. So the angrier a post or conversation is the more your focus is turned to it, keeping your emotions stoked and your eyeballs engaged.

This happens to me all the time at night. I will see someone respond to a post I put up, and I want to get back at them SO BAD. But I also needed to sleep, so I've been better at telling myself to put my phone down and get my ass in the sack.

Because of this biological response, it's really hard not to engage. But we all should try because this constant-fight garbage has consequences.

- Research shows fake news actually reaches more people than real news because it is new, raw, and generally makes people angry. So these posts get more clicks and shares. The more we live online, the more we're exposed to fraud.
- Conflict increases the amount of connection we feel with "our" group, be it gender, political parties, or sports teams. It also generates a feeling of superiority over the "other group." Stephen A Smith loves to poke at Dallas Cowboys fans because he knows he will get an angry response and therefore more engagement both from them and everyone else who likes hating them. Admit it, Cowboys fans, you're easily triggered.
- The angrier you are about something, the more likely you are to remember it. This keeps you wanting to engage more.

Look, a lot of us want to be angry because our brains get super amped when we fight, and those chemicals our bodies release can be addictive. Algorithms controlling the internet are set up to give you these fights. Anger is easily spread through networks of people, like online groups and chats. That emotion is then reinforced as people share more and more rage.

Companies know this. Leaked documents from Facebook show that corporate leaders know how much their program is increasing people's rage, but don't care because they also know all of that rage builds their bank accounts.

Bad for You

My dudes, being constantly online is TERRIBLE for your mental health.

- You are much more likely to compare yourself with others in negative ways. If all you see are all these snapshots of people with fast cars, hot girlfriends, and huge houses, you may look at what you've got and feel like shit even though you have no idea how accurate the posts are. It's like the sex in porn we talked about earlier: it ain't real, son.
- Being amped up all the time, like the internet wants you to be, makes it harder for you to sleep. And with less sleep, your brain gets less rest and more depressed.
- You know how your brain gets going over something, and can't let it go? Psychologists call it "rumination." For me, when I play as a goalkeeper for my soccer team and let in a bad goal, I go back to it over and over thinking how I could have done it better. The same thing happens with social media rumination, where you constantly think about your posts, comments, and other interactions. It is super common among young people and, again, leads to more stress and depression.
- All of this is super addictive, and the earlier you start, the more hooked you are. It's like a drug, and now that companies are setting up chat bots and AI girlfriends to keep you online longer, it's getting worse. Being constantly online makes you angrier, less likely to think about your actions, more aggressive, and less

likely to interact with real people that can help you feel better.

Maybe the worst thing is all of that anger you get online might drive you to do dangerous stuff. There is this thing called the "online disinhibition effect," which makes you interact worse online than you would in person because you don't have any of the normal barriers that you'd face talking to someone for real. People online can't punch you in the face for calling them something dickish like they could if you told them the same thing in a parking lot. Fake names generally turn people into bigger assholes.

Getting into online circle jerks of rage can lead to real life, terrible consequences for our communities.

- In 2016, "Pizzagate," a conspiracy theory claiming that the Democratic party was linked to a child sex trafficking ring through places like pizza restaurants, became viral. Through 4chan and 8chan, two forums for assholes where people drag themselves into rabbit holes of hate, it spread like crazy. A guy reading these sites went and shot up a random pizza place in Washington DC, thinking he was going to save kids. He didn't, because there weren't any to save.
- In 2019, another guy drove eight hours from Dallas to El Paso to shoot up a Walmart because he wanted to kill as many brown people as possible. He was a constant user of 8chan, where he posted his manifesto claiming he wanted to defend the U.S. against a "Hispanic Invasion." The result was 23 dead people.

- The guy who killed Charlie Kirk in 2025 had etched sayings on his bullet casings. One of them, "Notices bulge OwO what's this," is from online "furry" communities and is only known by those living deeply on the net.
- On the same day, a 16-year-old kid shot two people at a Colorado high school and then killed himself. He was active on a violent gore website called "Watch People Die." He also posted TikTok videos of himself putting together tactical gear while videos of previous mass shootings played in the background. Commentators told him how cool he was, and encouraged him to "make a move."

What to do?

Getting offline and into real life is better for you, but because of this chemical addiction, it can be really hard. Here are some things you can try, but you don't have to do everything all at once. Maybe do one or two things to start and then work your way up to other steps from there.

1. Delete your most addictive apps, or at least turn off your notifications for them. Constant reminders of interactions keep you glued to social media. But those things can wait, and making sure you are only online when you want to be keeps you sane.
2. Try to keep your phone out of some "real life" spaces, like your bedroom. I used to keep my phone by the bed as a clock, alarm, and white noise generator at night, but I was constantly scrolling. So, I got an old school

alarm clock and fan. Now my phone stays in another room charging while I sleep. It's...nice.

3. Speaking of which, get other non-online things to help with your life stuff. Now that phones are starting to be banned in schools, teens are getting a ton of analog watches to tell the time.

4. Try to set times during the day to use or not use. For instance, a "no phone thirty minutes before bed rule" works. "Batch check in times" when you can respond to texts or scroll online at specific times let you spend your other parts of the day living.

5. Build tolerance for being offline again. Try getting into a book or guitar, and when you feel a need to grab your phone, reach for your new hobby instead. Or, go for a walk without your headphones once in a while.

6. DO THINGS IN REAL LIFE. Austin Trout, the boxer who wrote the Foreword, once told me he loves young people getting into his gym and putting on gloves because, for that time, they can't be on their phone. Going to a movie, a real comedy club, or playing a game with friends gets the same result. And sure, use your phone to set up these meets. The reward is actual human interactions where your phone can stay in your pocket.

Fellas, getting offline and into real life will make you healthier, happier, and more stable. Maybe hit up a coffee shop or bar and strike up a conversation with a girl. You never know what might happen, and it beats the hell out of turning into a psychotic rage monster who shoots up a movie theatre, church, or school.

CHAPTER 17

Anger and Other Emotions

In the last chapter, we talked about how social media companies use our tendency for rage and conflict to keep us glued to our phones. This is a worse problem with guys because so many of us haven't been allowed to express the full range of emotions a human has. This is a tough subject to talk about, but it's important. So let's get to it.

Dudes can express joy, but only in the context of sports as fans. Think Bills Mafia. Fans can jump through all the tables they want or cry when they finally get to a playoff game.

In almost every other situation, men are encouraged to be apathetic, stoic, and otherwise emotionally restrained. Otherwise, if you show emotion, you are weak. Crying seems to be the worst offense.

Caleb Williams, Heisman Trophy winner, 1st overall draft pick of the Bears, and recent NFL semifinalist, cried with his mom after losing a critical game at USC. He was criticized for being "weak," "fragile," and was told there is "no crying in football." John Boehner, former Republican U.S. Speaker of the House, was repeatedly mocked for crying in defense of his wife from public attacks and when attending a speech by the pope.

But it doesn't stop there.

- Pro Bowl Cowboys Quarterback Dak Prescott openly talks about his struggles with depression and his brother's suicide. Pundits said he was showing "weakness."
- Steve Balmer, the world's 7th richest man, was called *Mr. Monkey Boy* after a joyful, passionate presentation at a Microsoft convention where he talked about his love for the company.
- BTS K-pop band members are labeled as "girly" for putting on flamboyant, emotional shows and wearing eyeliner.
- Howard Dean's campaign for President in 2004 was completely derailed after an energetic campaign rally, where his "Dean Scream" was labeled unpresidential and overly emotional.

In America, repressing the fuck out of our emotions starts early. Stephanie Behlke, a school teacher and PhD candidate at BYU studying how boys develop emotionally, describes a conversation in her elementary school class: "When I asked one of my current classes what vulnerability was, a boy in the back immediately piped up and said, 'Weakness.'" Her observation is backed up by research, in which a fear of weakness is found over and over in conversations with boys and young men.

This sucks. But the situation is made worse because we ARE allowed to express one thing at any time, in any place: rage.

Anger is a *manly* emotion that isn't looked down on, because it looks "strong." When Kobe Bryant would get in angry fights in games or in practice, he was labeled "intense," fearless, and showing his "Mamba mentality." Bernie Sanders is constantly described as "righteous" in his angry speeches about the woes of capitalism. Donald Trump is almost always angry. I mean, has anyone ever heard him laugh? His supporters say it shows that he cares, telling the truth "straight from the heart." Elon Musk, known for angry rants and rage firing, is praised for his "demanding leadership style."

Men's anger is seen as a show of strength, honesty, and focus. It's almost never bad, and this is backed up by more research. Male job applicants who display anger rather than sadness are praised and are more likely to be hired. Dudes who express anger on juries are more likely to influence other jurors to their view on a verdict. In the military, anger that crosses certain thresholds can be seen as a positive leadership trait in intense situations.

The message is simple. Hey man, you want to show a normal emotion? Crying? Joy? Depression? Sadness? You are feminine. A beta. A pussy.

But when you get angry? You are honest. Demanding. Focused. A leader.

Look, I *like* getting angry. When I was in politics, it felt so good to get nice and pissed off when I was fighting the good fight because that feeling is pure. It's clean. It's easy. And it gives you energy. When I get ready to go play goalkeeper in a soccer game, I listen to angry music before I get my gloves on because it gets me focused due to all those chemicals we talked about last chapter.

I will also admit, I'm terrible at expressing other emotions. My father never once told me he loved me or was proud of anything I did. Even though I knew he did and he was, I grew up with that as a model for how to be a man. Plus, middle and high school were just like the teacher described earlier. Don't want to fight? Cry sometimes? Express emotions through shit like poetry and songs? You are weak. Play football? Conquer those around you through anger and mockery? You are strong, and a role model.

The language of therapists is also super annoying to me. They use words like "hold space," "containers" of safety, setting boundaries, and having "trauma" from being "triggered."

When I hear that stuff, I just want to punch someone in the face. Why can't I just power through my shit and get back to work? Why should I take time dealing with this head stuff? It's fucking complicated, and hard to understand. Being sad sucks. I hate crying myself, and don't like hearing someone else do it.

Plus, I LIKE MY RAGE. It pumps me up, and feels good. Why can't I just have that all the time? I think a lot of men out there probably feel the same way.

But here's the thing, fellas. We need to find a way to put aside this bullshit, me included. Why?

It is bad for our bodies.

- The more we repress negative feelings like being sad or disappointed, the higher our cholesterol gets.

That leads to more heart attacks, strokes, and fucked-up kidneys.

- Men who are shitty processors of emotion get more stressed in bad situations than those who have a healthy relationship to their feelings.
- Those of us who don't process emotions well get less and worse sleep.
- We tend to get sicker, and it is harder to process the food we eat. So if you want to build up that body, repressing emotions makes it harder to digest that protein.

And that is just the non-brain stuff. Screwed-up emotions are just as bad as a long-term injury.

- Every time we push down our emotions, like sadness, the more likely we are to become depressed right away.
- Trying to balance out negative emotions with things like being "self-reliant," having power over women, or living the life of a "playboy" only makes things worse.
- Research shows the longer we do this, the better chance we have to die of heart disease and even cancer.
- Drug addiction becomes more common for dudes who keep all of our real emotions clamped down.
- When we cannot fucking face all of our emotions head on, we are more likely to kill ourselves. And remember dude, I've been there.

It's also really important to remember that the more we don't man up and get ourselves right with our feelings, the more consequences there are for everyone around us. How?

- The better we are at crushing how we feel, the worse we are at things like first impressions, having good people around to support us, and keeping quality women around for any length of time.
- Stress from emotional repression turns to anger and we become a lot more likely to hit someone, like the woman or kid in our lives.
- The more pressure we are under to not express ourselves, the more likely we are to become a monster. Remember, 97% of mass shooters are dudes. Most of them experienced rejection that led to bad feelings, and they kept their shit bottled up until they exploded.

If we *really* want to be strong, and not like all the guys we see on the TV after they shot up a church or school, it means we have to take on the hard stuff and do real work. Just because something isn't solved by being able to hit it or push it away doesn't mean it ain't hard. Doing this work is so uncomfortable, because we have to take a real, honest look at ourselves.

But we're not supposed to be afraid of a little hard work, right? Sci-fi author Brandon Sanderson writes about a combat vet who is trying to be better at this mental health and emotional stuff. He describes these efforts by saying they are "warrior thoughts." So maybe think of it that way.

Because so many fellas have repressed this shit since we were kids, a lot of us don't even know what it is when we feel sadness, grief, joy, or pride. Pros call this "emotional literacy," and this means you have to really focus on how you are feeling at the time to recognize it. Try some of these things to get better at it:

- Be present. That means really paying attention to the people around you. Concentrate on how they are feeling. Don't judge them, and then use that process to think about what that might make you feel. Teddy Bridgewater, longtime NFL backup QB, recently did a commercial where he came in as a "backup listener." It's brilliant, but he also shows how to really concentrate on the people you are with.
- Explore how it feels to express emotion other than anger to people you know and trust. It doesn't have to be negative. My sister has done serious work in the past year with her boyfriend's kids, and it's showing. They are starting to trust her. I recently told her how proud I was of her for this, and her face just lit up in this amazing smile. I felt really good about giving her some joy.
- Make sure you are putting work into seeing friends you like on the regular. Keep them around by doing things in real life with them.
- Don't be afraid to take some time during the day to reflect on how you feel about things. Some people like to journal, but for people like me who don't, try reflecting on your drive home, walking the dog, or while getting that yard work done on the weekend. If something stressed you out or made you really happy, those are normal things. Try and figure out what made each happen, why you felt that way, and

what it means to you.

- BREATHE. I know, just focusing on your breath can seem hippie dippy. But I'm telling you, it fucking works. Take some time (even a minute) to just breathe, focusing on that and what comes into your head and then letting that go. It is a good way to get familiar with how you are feeling.

Lastly, don't be an asshole when some other guy expresses emotion. Men aren't pussies or betas for crying, weak for talking about depression, or unstable just because they have some joy. Being a better person for them will make you more comfortable with yourself. Plus, you'll be happier and less likely to get on those drugs, beat up someone, die from a heart attack, or kill yourself.

Adam Morisson was a star player for Gonzaga's 2006 Sweet 16 team that lost to UCLA. They were up the whole game, but couldn't score in the last few minutes and lost by two at the buzzer. Morrison became famous for crying on the court, and when asked about it later had an amazing response.

"Yeah, I cried. I cried on national TV. So what? Failure hurts. I'll cry again. I hope I never lose that intensity."

The dude understood what he was feeling, why he was sad, and wasn't embarrassed about it. He also is an NBA Champion as one of Kobe's teammates on the 2010 Lakers.

Let's all try and be a little more like that.

CHAPTER 18

Men and the Economy

Earlier in this book, we talked about the disappearance of traditional manufacturing careers and how that's been hard on men in the job market. Free trade lowered costs and created new jobs across the country, but it stopped many men from being able to get long-term, well-paying work without a degree. Unfortunately, with the combination of AI, robots, and lower education rates, many men are choosing to give up on this economy.

Feeling stuck in terms of work and not being able to afford rent and food makes all our feelings of loneliness, frustration, and anger even worse. And if we don't take the issue up head on, it is only going to get worse.

Dudes and Work

There's no other way to put this. We have a problem.

In 1960, almost every guy who could get a job, did. But since then, there has been a steady increase in the number

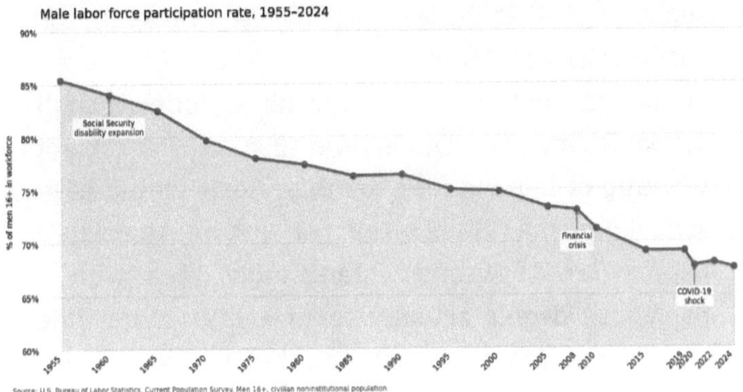

of fellas who can work, but don't.

That number is now close to forty million men complete-ly out of the labor force.

This isn't the unemployment rate, which has remained pretty low since we got out of COVID. That number only measures everyone who doesn't have a job AND is looking for one. If you just give up, your ass on the couch doesn't count. Even though the forty million number includes stu-dents and retirees, still, the number of dudes who feel so left out that they aren't even looking for work is staggering. So who are these guys? They are younger, either black or white, and less educated.

- While men of almost all ages are dropping in their work rates, young men in the 16-24 age bracket are the highest group choosing to sit on the couch. 64% were in the job market in 2014. Now? That number is only 56%.
- When race is measured, 79% of Hispanic/Latino men are working followed by 75% of Asian men. White (70%) and Black (69%) men trail behind by a lot, which

sucks given that these groups together make up the vast majority of U.S. dudes.

- Education matters. Dudes who never finished high school spend way more time (23% of weeks) not working or looking for a job than those with a high school diploma (15% of weeks) or with an Associate's Degree (11% of weeks). Interestingly, men with a Bachelor's degree actually spent a little more time out of work (14% of weeks) even though women with the same education were working more. We'll get into the reason later.

Now the real question. *Why* are these guys sitting on a couch instead of working?

- As we discussed, there has been a huge decline in manufacturing and energy jobs traditionally held by dudes without higher levels of education.
- Robots and other types of automation have gotten better in recent years, and even adding only one robot per thousand workers lowers jobs created and wages earned. In 2023 alone, there were over 44k new robots installed in U.S. factories.
- Wages have also dropped for people with lower levels of education. In the '70s, workers with high school diplomas made 80% of the salary of someone with a BA. But by the mid 2010's, that number was down to 60%. And men have been less and less likely than women to stay in class past high school.
- Marriage rates are down significantly for everyone. Less than half of American adults are now hitched,

and people that do get married are doing so later in life. Why does this matter? Studies show that married men have a higher incentive to work. At the same time, fewer good jobs available for men decreases marriage rates. These pressures contribute to the downward spiral of dudes not working.

- Among developed countries, we have the highest number of people in prison (almost all men) and it's not even close. A criminal record makes it much harder to get and keep a job.
- Video games have increased in quality while becoming much cheaper. 72% of young American men say they play them often or sometimes, and as games have gotten better the number of hours young men work has dropped. This isn't just a work thing. They are even choosing games more over sex.
- Drug addiction (especially opioids) and suicide among men have been on the rise, showing that more of us are depressed and less motivated to work.
- A lack of affordable housing options and declining wages have led more young men to live at home. When this happens, even though they save money, they are less motivated to go find work.

Men and Women

When I was New Mexico's Labor Secretary, I noticed something during the COVID pandemic. Many of the jobs shut down, like construction, manufacturing, and oil drilling, were in industries with more dudes. However, things like hospitals and schools, areas where the vast majority of workers are women, kept going. The effects haven't stopped with COVID. Currently, unemployment for young women is only around 7% while the rate for young men is at 9%.

Why? Women tend to pursue jobs that involve helping people, while men tend to like work that involves stuff and systems. This trend hurts men.

While we know robots are eating into manufacturing job opportunities, artificial intelligence is having the same effect on other types of jobs dudes gravitate to. Men make up almost 80% of American Computer Science majors. But since 2022, almost 25% of entry level coding jobs have disappeared because AI programs can do that work better and cheaper. 75-80% of certified financial planners are men. Studies are now showing, though, that computer programs are more accurate, able to handle complexity better, and that many men are already trusting AI with their portfolios more than real people.

Meanwhile, it is really hard to replicate jobs in healthcare with robots or AI for two reasons. First, while some of the business/admin roles in health care might be eventually replaced, it is really hard to artificially replace hands-on workers like phlebotomists. Second, health care is an emotional business that requires empathy and connection. A robot or AI program might be great at making cars or predicting the future of the stock market. But they cannot give a human being comfort at a time when they are scared about their health. Only a person can.

The same thing can be said for education, another area dominated by women. A chatbot cannot by its nature replicate the interaction and mentoring that a human teacher can, and will therefore be less effective in teaching our kids.

This helps explain the difference between employment levels for men and women with Bachelor's degrees. If men are getting theirs in areas that don't require human interaction, well, those jobs might not be there in the near future. Women, though, are getting degrees in things like health care and education where those jobs WILL be around.

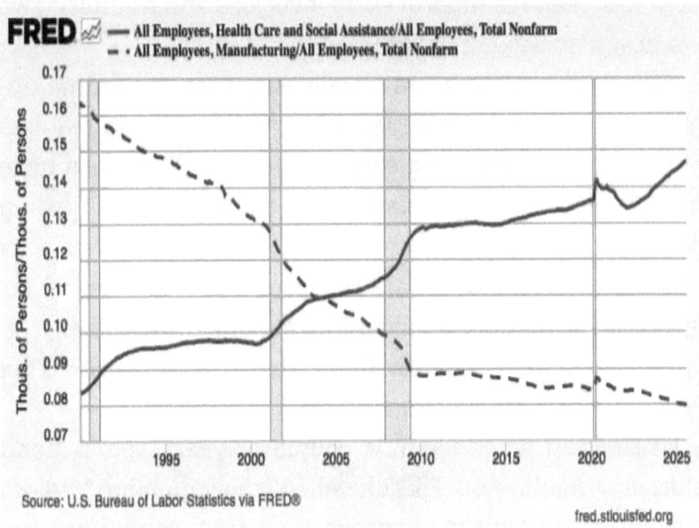

It's also interesting to note that while non-married men are less likely to have a job, women are the opposite. 64.3% of never-married women are working, while both separated (64%) and divorced (61%) women were more likely to work than married ones (59%).

One reason women who want careers are less likely to get or stay married? Many husbands create tension in marriages when their wives focus on their careers. Need a good example? In relationships where the woman makes more money than the dude, they do MORE of the household chores and are more likely to be victims of domestic violence.

This isn't a great incentive to get married.

Not Just Men

To be fair, the job market has been harder for all young people to navigate, regardless of gender. AI is now regularly used to screen resumes of entry level jobs and AI interviews are now also becoming standard.

Applicants almost universally say that the online application process for many jobs is complicated and requires a ton of time formatting each application. More jobs have multiple levels of interviews, and algorithms are turning down people they see as overqualified. On the other edge of the sword, employers are requiring more experience. So, how does a younger applicant go about getting the experience needed for a job, without the ability to land a job in the first place? Tough question.

It's gotten so bad that a couple of years ago, a trend started spreading on TikTok called "rage applying," where people just apply for every job they find, sometimes using those same AI tools that companies use to screen new applicants. This, among other things, has led to a lack of feedback on their status which has left young people even more pissed off.

Bright Spot

There is one real bright spot for young dudes' jobs right now: the trades.

Over 380,000 new jobs will show up in the next decade to build houses, put in those new wind turbines, and update our transportation network. One in three U.S. bridges needs replacement, many of the country's biggest airports are either now or will soon be starting major renovations, and numerous highway projects are slated to start soon.

Plus, all of those new data centers powering the AI programs forecasting the stock market, coding new computer programs, and screening your resume? Welders, diesel mechanics, HVAC technicians, and electricians are needed to build and maintain them.

Last year, 91,000 more people attended two-year career technical education courses, keeping up a trend that has seen a 20% growth since 2020. Most of these courses are in areas like HVAC and welding, which tend to be overwhelmingly male.

Apprenticeships, where students get a paycheck for work during the day while attending class a couple of nights a week, have been spreading like wildfire. Many of these jobs have been in union shops, where workers are able to get better paychecks and have a place to connect with other guys, which is so rare these days.

Despite these opportunities, we still have work to do. Next, we'll examine what we should and shouldn't be doing to help fellas get better employment opportunities, which will help with all of the other parts of their lives.

Hint: this does NOT include trying to go back to a fantasy time with things like tariffs or putting women "back in their place" as baby-makers and homemakers to reduce competition for jobs. Arresting every brown person on sight because they are "taking our jobs" isn't going to help either.

It does include people on the left acknowledging the problem, employers increasing wages across the board, helping more men get into education programs in the jobs that will be around (*and making sure they graduate*), building more housing so young people have the opportunity for an affordable place to live, and getting rid of some of the stupid, sexist barriers that have men choosing NOT to go into the people-centric jobs that will be around.

It's a shit ton of stuff. But we can do it if we put our minds to it.

CHAPTER 19

Interviews with Interesting Guys

SIDDEEQ SHABAZZ

Dr. Siddeeq Shabazz played football when he was young. A running back in high school, he walked on at New Mexico State before earning a scholarship. Willing to change positions, he started as a running back but shifted to defense and ended up playing safety and linebacker for four years in college and then seven years as a professional. He suited up for the Raiders, Falcons, and Saints while also playing in Germany and Canada.

Siddeeq didn't stop growing when he left the game though. Deciding that his intellectual growth was critical to becoming a better man, he went back to school and earned a PhD in Business Administration. His research focuses on how service employees influence customers. He factors in emotions and justice issues to regular business practices. Spiritual meaning also is critical to him, and he has worked to evolve positively in that aspect of his life as well.

A thoughtful, introspective man with many diverse experiences, he has some fascinating lessons to share about sports, education, and getting better as a man.

Role Models

"My stepfather was in the military. He was a disciplinarian. He would do all the spanking but we didn't have much interaction with him. He would go to work before the sun came up, and he would come home when the sun came down, and I didn't interact with him unless I had to go serve him his food, his lemonade that I had to make, or get reprimanded for cutting up in school or getting in trouble on the property, not doing my chores or something. He was also an eighth-degree black belt in martial arts, so the only real time that I had with him was Thursdays and Saturdays every day of my childhood. We had at least an hour, hour and a half, of karate class that was open to the public. So as a role model, I think I've always had role models of what not to be, what I didn't want to be."

Football Players

"I personally thought of most football players, college and especially at the professional level, as just a caricature of a man who plays football. And what I was impressed by was the diversity of men in every locker room that I was in, the diversity of intelligence, the diversity of creativity, the diversity of interests and backgrounds. And we pigeonhole our idea of [football players], especially the black athlete, as something that's totally distorted. I was super impressed by so many intelligent white and especially black men who make it to that level. And what I kind of realized was that the stigma around being a black male athlete is so twisted and so messed up. And that's part of where I'm at today. I would love to show that I'm not an anomaly. There's so many intelligent players that you don't see.

"I hear so many people, especially Caucasian non-athletes, degrade men of color at this level. They degrade 'em while they're playing and not performing well, then they degrade all of them when one person makes a mistake. And being that Black monolith is a weight that no man should have to carry. And I think far too many of us have to carry that because people are misinformed about who's really out there playing, who's really taking a knee or standing up or putting their hand on their heart when the American flag is being waved."

Getting a PhD

"This PhD was me showing my kids who I really am. It was giving them a narrative like, 'OK, my dad, he's not a one-trick pony. He's not just this, this football guy who ran around and messed around a lot. He's a dedicated person.' I wanted to show them what our last name meant through seeing me work hard while they were kids to get this PhD, and I wanted them to know they were around people who could show them that drive.

"I feel like I can always learn and be a better professor,

be better at teaching. And the opportunity to do research is really cool, and to be paid to learn and share what I do. I was doing that already as a coach, as a mentor, as a personal trainer, as a lifestyle coach. That's who I've been my whole life. So now getting paid to do it, it's just a great opportunity. So, I think having a job in academia is a blessing. At the high school and elementary level, you don't really see a whole lot of men. But there's a great opportunity to pour into the next generation."

Value of Counseling

"I've been doing a lot of work in this arena over the last few years. Never really wanted to do counseling. But I got into a position in life, going through a separation and trying to salvage my marriage, and invested everything I could into salvaging that marriage, which meant thousands of dollars on counseling. Counseling I didn't think I needed because on my resume I achieved a lot of things that I put my mind to.

"And I'm thankful for this lesson. I think I'm a new man three years later through understanding how my childhood impacted my today, how it impacted my marriage, all of my relationships, and how now I've done some healing to create a new story moving forward. This transition that I've been going through, going through divorce, and really trying to heal and heal in a deep way for the first time."

Faith

"I struggle saying I'm a Christian. I say it all the time, but what I really mean is I'm a Christ follower because I'm so scared of being lumped in with this group of people that I do not believe really are interacting with the world the way that we're called to. So, this hypocrisy? I think it's emboldened by somebody like Trump. I see how Trump has really created this weird flip back to like, how white people have always been able to treat women and diverse people from diverse backgrounds. And I think that's what Trump invigorated in this culture and even a lot of men who I don't think walk out their faith as much as they talk about their faith."

Strength and Weakness

"I'm becoming somebody who apologizes to my friends a lot more, my family, when I make mistakes. And that model, the conquer model, there's no apologies. Trump? No apologies. I think that's for weak people, weak men who are battling just to have a little confidence in their life. But a real man, who's confident in their ability or confident that there's a better way, I think it's gonna come to being vulnerable enough to be real. Be real about the things that you're not good at and the

things that you are good at. A guy like Trump, they hide their weaknesses, and their weaknesses will always be weaknesses.

"A man like me? With a growth mindset? My weakest point is the weakest point. And that's gonna be my place where I break. And I feel like I finally started to touch on the weakest points that I was so scared to talk to people about when it came to just emotions, sexuality, the abuse that I experienced. And being able to get through the other side of that? That's no longer a stopping point for me, and I feel like I'm at this launching point in my life. I played in the NFL, I have a PhD, and I feel like I'm barely about to launch in my life. There's more to come. I'm excited about the future, not just for me. The launching is in showing other men how to take hold of all the tragedy in their life, all the fear, all the mistakes, and turn it into something powerful. What we see Trump's doing, what we see these conquer-all guys doing, it's not life-changing. I've changed my one life. Now I wanna have impact on others, and it comes through relationships, not accumulating things for myself."

CHAPTER 20

Institutional Responsibility for a Better Male Economy

Having an understanding about where men are economically is important, but just bitching about it doesn't solve anything either. So, what can communities do to actually help men? There are awesome concrete things, and here's a look at some of them.

Costs of a College Education

Over the past few decades, getting a Bachelor's degree has been the best way to set yourself up for a good life with a good job. For men, though, this has started to change. We've already mentioned that for the first time, getting a BA isn't guaranteeing a better life for men. While part of that is on dudes, and the types of jobs that are going to be around, another reason is the cost of a college education.

In 1981, the average tuition for a four-year degree at a public college was about $12k. Today that cost is about $25k, doubling inflation rates for everything else. Combine that with skyrocketing prices for things like food and housing and the result is most of us dudes don't think it's a good choice. Only 22% of adults think going to college is worth the time if you have to take out loans, which most people need. 70% of graduates with a Bachelor's today have some debt when they graduate.

That means one simple thing. If universities want to stay relevant as the economy changes, they have to cut their damn costs. The problem? There isn't a ton of incentive.

When I was student government president at New Mexico State in 2000-2001, one of my big achievements was pushing the state legislature to fully fund the state's lottery scholarship. It gave any high school graduate in the state free tuition if they went right to college. Schools, though, upped their tuition like crazy every year because they figured, "What the hell? The state is going to cover it, so we can get more money in."

That didn't last though, because lottery money stopped growing about thirteen years later, which meant the law had to change so kids only got a percentage of tuition covered with the state's help. I was elected to the State Legislature in 2012 and had to vote on this shit in 2013, which was a buzzkill considering how much energy I put into the idea back in 2001.

This same issue exists across the country as schools think a never-ending supply of help from the government will always be there. So they keep upping tuition costs to fund a couple of things. The two biggest internal reasons for rising costs at schools? Too many administrators, and building huge new shit for students.

Yale has more administrative staff now than they do

actual students. Though that's an extreme example, colleges spend an average of around $4500 per student in a year on people that don't work on academics. Some of these folks are needed, but if colleges truly want to be more affordable, they have to cut down on the positions that aren't contributing to students' education. I mean, I worked in college fundraising for a bit and there were four associate deans in the office.

Four. That's crazy.

Schools also think they have to compete for students by building shiny new things. Think fancy dorms, big ass dining halls, and gyms with huge climbing walls. Texas Tech even has a lazy river. I'm not saying going to school shouldn't be fun, but universities aren't fucking water parks.

Schools are in an "arms race" to recruit new students and keep their numbers up, so they feel they need to add all of this stuff to lure kids in. But if colleges don't internally recognize that young people today, and *especially young men*, think college is too expensive, they will keep seeing their numbers drop.

An educated population is better for all of us, producing better jobs and healthier communities. Cities with a higher number of people with four-year degrees are also safer. So let's do what we can to get more guys who want four-year degrees into and through school by laying off things like new water parks and cutting tuition.

Completing Education

While many men don't choose a traditional, four-year school, they are choosing to join trade schools and apprenticeships. This is great! We need more people working with their hands, and unlike manufacturing, many of these jobs in construction will be hard to replace with a robot.

Here's the thing, though. Men and boys aren't completing their education. In every state that records rates by gender, more girls graduated than boys. This ranges from a 2% gap in North Dakota to a 9% gap in Mississippi. If you want to go into trades, you need that piece of paper. Community colleges and most apprenticeships won't take you without it.

Men who do go to college drop out at a higher level than women, including for Associate's degrees that can lead to jobs in the trades. Most apprenticeships in the U.S. are still focused on male-dominated trades, but only about two in three complete their training.

That isn't good enough. If a guy makes the decision to get into school, and then drops out, what have we accomplished? For many, only a huge waste of time and money.

Luckily, there are a ton of things schools, governments, and organizations can do to help in these crucial areas. Here are a few we can think about:

More Men in Education

Only 23% of U.S. public school teachers are men. This has real effects on boys. Yes, boys are generally given more attention in class, but this isn't always a good thing. They are way more resistant to formal instruction (skipping class, arguing, etc.), twice as many boys than girls are getting suspended or expelled, punishments for boys are stronger, girls are performing better in class, and almost ¾ of high school valedictorians are now girls.

We need more male role models in K-12 education, as

research shows that boys learn better from other dude teachers. If schools don't have a balance of men and women teaching, it's a good bet boys will continue to fall behind.

In North Carolina and California, when minority male community college students were assigned a success coach and/or mentors to help with their issues, there was an 8% increase in retention rates. When schools and trades programs engage with young men to find out what they need, and then help them get those things, more guys complete their education. Is it extra tutoring in class? Money for equipment? Some leeway when they have kids and need to be there for their families?

Every program in the U.S. should be asking these questions and coming up with solutions that allow more guys to get their certificates, apprenticeships, or Associate's degrees.

Support Organizations

Organizations for women that provide support, mentorship, and education are everywhere. And it's important to remind us all that this was necessary because of the roadblocks placed in front of them for decades. From manufacturing, to STEM and tech, to engineering, and accounting, there are support groups for women in a ton of traditionally male-dominated fields. And they have been very successful, which is why we see more and more women in many of these fields.

Where, then, are the support structures for men?

Unions have been the traditional places where men could get educated and then find work in construction and manufacturing. But union membership has been down for a while and continues to decline. For dudes in traditionally female jobs (the ones dealing with people,) there is an American Association for Men in Nursing, and there are some decent orgs for black men in teaching. These are the exceptions to the rule. Plus, they're much smaller than the organizations for their female counterparts.

If we really want a better situation for men in the job market, we should take a page from the ladies' book; get more guys into unions while creating places for dudes to support one another in job areas we know will be around for a while.

Build Shit

American infrastructure is falling behind. Roads are crumbling, bridges are collapsing, and many places in the U.S. don't have good internet.

- Almost 20% of U.S. dams have a "high hazard potential," meaning people living below them are at risk of getting hurt by floods.
- 39% of U.S. roads are in poor condition, causing more crashes. This means injuries, death, and a ton more money needed to fix our cars.
- 7% of our bridges are in "poor" condition. If they aren't fucking fixed, we'll have more issues like the recent horrendous collapses in Philly and Baltimore.
- More electric cars and reliance on data centers for our online stuff means we will need double the electricity by 2030 than we are demanding now. So if we don't get more power AND the cables we need to get power everywhere, your electric bills will go way up.

- 10% of U.S. houses don't have a broadband internet subscription, either wired or through their phones. This means those folks don't have the education, health care, and shopping resources they need for a 21st Century economy.

All of this lagging infrastructure sucks. So what can we do about it? More money and less red tape.

Joe Biden, who had plenty of faults, actually hit a home run when he got the Infrastructure and Jobs Act pushed in 2021. It gave over $500 Billion to fund 40,000 projects like repairing roads, building bridges, connecting homes to the internet, etc. Employment of heavy and civil engineers was up 9% two years after, and construction jobs were up 11%.

That's a lot of fucking jobs for dudes. We should do more of that.

The Federal government needs to look at all of their regulations and get rid of the ones that stop us from building. Research shows that the U.S. lags behind other places around the world in building public infrastructure. Two of the main causes are complicated environmental reviews and public comment times that take WAY too long.

Don't get me wrong, we need good environmental regulations. However, massive delays are killing projects and driving up the cost. The ironic thing is that many of the environmentalists who defend these regulations are killing construction projects in areas like green energy and mass transit that we need to fight climate change.

The same can be said for public comment. In Spain, they have six-week timeframes where people can let the builders of whatever project know what they think. Here, the process can take years. People should have the ability to give their opinion, but they need to do so efficiently.

The problem with both of these issues is this: *time is fucking money*. The longer things take, the higher the cost. The more expensive they are, the less taxpayers get for their money. The less we get, the angrier we are and the less we want to do. When that happens, traffic goes up, bridges collapse, dams fail, and we run out of electricity. *And no jobs are created in sectors where a lot of dudes traditionally hold the jobs.*

Housing

The infrastructure problem doesn't stop there. America has a massive housing crisis. Prices are up, as are mortgage rates and insurance premiums, but sales are down. Young renters face huge problems as the cost of rent keeps climbing. There is a 7.1 million homes shortage for the working people who need a roof over their heads the most. Homelessness is at a record high.

This is hitting young men. Hard.

25.7% of men between the ages of 25-29 still live at home with their parents. Only 17.7% of women the same age do. In the 30-34 age group, men are almost twice as likely to still be living at home. 75% of young men who earn less than $25,000 per year are what is called "cost burdened" (meaning they spend more than 50% of their monthly income on rent). And as marriage rates for young people continue to fall, single guys find affordable housing harder to get than married ones. For a $300,000 home, someone needs to make about $61,000 per year, but only 43% of single men bring in this salary yearly. Gen Z men actually rate buying a house as a higher priority than women, but the ladies are getting into more of them.

It's not rocket science. If I think it's important to own a home, but can't buy one even though the women around me are, I'm more likely to think society is stacked against me. If I really want to ask a girl out, but know that I'll eventually have to bring her back to my childhood home or my place with a million roommates, I may not even bother.

Cities and counties make rules on building homes. This is called zoning, and the concept is that you can only build houses in certain places with certain rules. For instance, I can only put apartments in one area, but in another place all the homes have to have huge lots. It's one of the biggest reasons more houses don't get built, which raises prices for everyone. However, these laws are being defended by people called NIMBYs. This stands for Not In My Backyard. Think of the person that says, "I am all for new apartments, trains, or windmills for electricity...just don't put them next to me."

If everyone says this and wins, shit doesn't get built anywhere.

If we really want to make things better for young men in terms of getting an affordable roof over their heads and creating more jobs, we have to build more. That means electing people to county and city boards who want to reform or get rid of zoning laws that restrict new housing, transportation, electricity, or other things for no good reason.

So, all of this is what schools, organizations, and governments can do to create better educational costs and job situations for dudes. But what can we do individually? In the next chapter, we'll look at some of those things.

◆

CHAPTER 21

What Dudes can do about Jobs and Bills

Now we've seen what governments, schools, and organizations can do to improve the economic situation for American men. But relying on someone else to do everything isn't what we're about.

So what can WE do to make sure we are getting to a good financial place?

Go to and finish School

Yes, more guys think school isn't worth the time or money. And yes, more of us feel the pull to work with our hands in a world where everything seems to be fake or online.

Here's the thing, though. In the 21st Century, we all need at least some education for almost anything we want to do. No one graduates from high school and gets a $100k job anymore. Want some examples?

In manufacturing, robots are now being used for menial shit because they "don't take lunch breaks, they don't demand overtime, and they don't get injured. They deliver parts to the right place at the right time, removing human error and delay." In new plants, robots are sorting parts, driving forklifts, and doing assembly. Experts believe that between 39-58% of jobs like these, currently done by people, could be replaced by some type of machine in the next ten years.

Are there still going to be manufacturing jobs for people? Sure, but they are going to be more technical. For instance, people who can fix these robots, work on 3D printers, make sure sensors function, and manage the networks that connect all of this stuff will absolutely be needed. But you can't just come in off the street and get one of these jobs. You have to know what the fuck you're doing. Many people won't get the skills they need, though, and it's why two million of these jobs could go unfilled in the next 8 years.

If you want to work on, say, 3D printers you are going to need a certificate like the CAMT (Certified Additive Manufacturing Technician). Training programs are offered at community colleges, and can take between three months to a year. They teach you stuff like how to work with the machines themselves, run their programming, use the right materials, and do everything safely.

Employers will also want you to have "soft skills," which means knowing how to work with people. If you can't communicate effectively with your team, solve problems without too much oversight, and use time effectively you're not going to be as competitive. You can learn those things with an Associate's Degree, which means you generally need at least two years of school.

And even when you get one of these jobs, that ain't it for your learning. Technology is changing so fast, and you'll want to keep up. "Stackable certificates" will let companies know you're willing to stay up to date. This will ensure you have a good paying job into the future. But you have to keep going to school to get them.

This stuff ain't just about manufacturing:

- Want a job as a welder? You'll need a certificate or community college degree.
- Electrician? A certificate plus an apprenticeship.
- Fix cars? They're complicated now. You'll need a one- to two-year degree, and a lot of places will want you to have an ASE (Automotive Service Excellence) certification.

So even if you don't want a Bachelor's degree, to earn you still have to learn.

Bachelor's Degree

My old man never pressured my sister or me on a profession when we left the house. But one thing was never in doubt: our asses were going to college for a four-year degree. He and his sister were the first people in their family to get them, and he said something to me when I was a kid that I will never forget.

"Bill, a lot of the stuff you learn in college, you won't use directly for a job. But you will learn how to learn, and people will want you for that."

As we talked about a couple of chapters ago, because of changes in AI, many jobs men like are being lost to computers. This has had a negative effect on employment of men, as guys with a BA are actually less likely to be working than dudes with an Associate's or even a high school degree right now.

However, there are still a lot of really good arguments to be made for biting the bullet and getting that full four-year degree. The biggest reason?

Show. Me. The Money.

Even with the slowdown in jobs, completing that Bachelor's degree means you will earn more. The average person with a high school degree makes $946 a week. If you've got some college or an Associate's Degree, that rises to $1,053. For those with that four-year degree, the number climbs to $1,533 per week.

That is not to say everyone who gets a BA always earns more than everyone who completes a certificate. My ex was a radiology tech with a two-year degree from a Community College, and I have a Master's from Harvard. For a while, she made way more than me when I was a State Representative ...but my degree allowed me the opportunity for a higher-paying job as a State Cabinet Secretary. When it happened, I pulled in substantially more.

One of the reasons you make more money with a full degree? Promotion. If you have a degree, you "are more than twice as likely as those without a degree to move to a position with higher degree requirements."

That's because my old man was right. Employers want people who have learned how to learn, and have the skills necessary to manage other people, communicate well, and handle budgets. You get a lot of skills and experiences with the full college trip that you may not get with just high school, a credential, or even an Associate's.

And it *doesn't have to be expensive*. At least ten U.S. states offer programs that can get you through four years of school for free, tuition-wise anyway. New York's Excelsior Scholarship, Minnesota's North Star Promise, Arizona's Promise program, Indiana's 21st Century Scholars, and New Mexico's Opportunity Scholarship are all options...if you take the challenge to get in and then keep your ass eligible with good grades.

For the straight guys reading this, there is another reason to think about getting the full college experience. Have you ever seen the original *Top Gun*? The one from the '80s? There is a scene where Tom Cruise's Maverick walks into a bar and points out all of the women around to his friend Goose (Anthony Edwards), calling it a "Target Rich Environment." Guess, what? College is the same thing right now.

There are about 15.4 million students in college. 58% of them, or 8.9 million, are women. 42%, or 6.5 million, are men.

That's almost 2-to-1, fellas.

Yes, I am saying that a university could be a great place to meet a girl.

And it's not just about the ratio. Women are saying, more and more, that they want to date a guy with a degree. 63% of them consider educational level very important when they go out with a dude. They are going to school and want someone they can talk and relate to. So you can hit the weights and get ripped, but if you really want to make a girl happy don't forget to work that upstairs part of your body as well.

Be Open to ALL Professions

My friend Jon is a nurse anesthetist. He got a four-year Bachelor's degree, then a Masters specializing in anesthesia. He helps people go under and come safely out when they need a big surgery.

He has a happy marriage, a couple of cute kids, and is always posting about trips he takes to see games or visit beaches. The dude is having a really good time. He also is very open and honest about how he keeps a family going in a house with two full-time working parents (his wife is also a nurse anesthetist).

Jon chose wisely. The average salary for his gig is $111.39 an hour. That's $231,700 per year. And he'll work for as long as he wants, wherever he feels like living. There will be about 33,000 new job openings in his field every year for the next decade.

Like other health care jobs, women are choosing these

jobs more than men. Only about 40% of nursing positions in Jon's specific field are filled by dudes. While that is a pretty stark difference, most health care gigs have WAY more women.

- Registered nurses make $93k per year, with almost 190k new job openings expected each year. Only about 12% of these jobs, though, are held by men.
- Radiology techs make about $90k per year with over 15k expected new positions needed each year. Only about 32% are dudes.
- Phlebotomists only need a short training certificate, and still make about $44k per year. Lots of those gigs (about 20k) are going to be needed every year, but only 16% of these jobs are filled by guys.

Dental assistants and hygienists, speech pathologists, mental health therapists, and teachers are all good, needed gigs that pay a decent salary. But all of them are dominated by women.

It turns out, many girls decide during high school that they want to go into HEAL jobs; health, education, and literacy. Almost a third of boys don't know what they want to do at that age, and the ones that do tend to want jobs dealing with stuff. Think STEM, business management, and manual labor.

The HEAL jobs women are choosing? Again, they're not likely to be replaced by AI or robots anytime soon. This leaves a ton of guys at a disadvantage.

What gives? Why are most guys not choosing these jobs?

Turns out a lot of the reason goes back to the issues we

talk about with men's emotions. These jobs require you to be warm, caring, and able to deal with others personally in emotional times. However, these qualities are still seen as "feminine" and therefore seen by many men as a form of weakness. The result? We don't apply for these jobs, no matter how many workers are needed or how good the pay is.

Unfortunately, when some of us do try one of these career paths, we can be treated poorly. Studies show many people don't trust a man who gets a job taking care of young kids, and dudes who do teach in elementary school report feeling lonely and isolated. Some patients view dude nurses as less skilled versus ladies doing the same job, and there are even cases where people have refused male nurses for their care. The result? Only one in four men who enter a female dominated field after coming from either a male dominated or neutral one end up sticking around.

But, fellas, there is another problem here and it has nothing to do with emotional expression or how we're treated. It turns out, when women start getting into a certain type of job, men just...leave.

98% of U.S. veterinarians were dudes in 1960. Now? Over 70% of vets and almost 80% of vet school graduates today are ladies. In the early '70s, men made up almost half of U.S. social workers. That number has been declining, and is now around 20%. CPAs used to be almost all men. Now? Over 60% of positions are held by women.

This shit is called "male flight," and it doesn't have a ton to do with money or job security. We just see "feminine" jobs as "lesser," full stop. This is a bad situation, as women don't seem to have as much of a problem with "our" jobs. There's been increasing participation in all of those above fields plus professions like doctors, attorneys, and business managers.

If we aren't OK with even thinking about trying a gig just because more of the workers are women, we are going to keep suffering. That needs to change.

Women Bosses

The business manager thing brings up another problem. When I was New Mexico Labor Secretary, a friend told me about this great, young female attorney who might be interested in the gig as our top legal counsel. I hired her, and she was amazing: super smart, worked really hard, cared about the people we were responsible for, and fit in great with the rest of our management team. It was one of my better decisions.

One of the lawyers that was already there, though? He had a problem. In his early sixties, he constantly questioned her decisions and didn't get work done that she assigned him to do. I finally had a Come to Jesus with him, saying if he couldn't work under her direction, then he either needed to retire or we would have to move him somewhere else. I learned a few days later from a co-worker that he went home and talked to his wife, complaining that he just couldn't take direction from a young woman.

We ended up having to transfer him. He just couldn't do it.

He's not the only dude, though, that has issues working for women. Research shows that:

- Many men feel threatened by a woman in a position

of power over them.
- Men are way more likely to interrupt and "mansplain" to female co-workers (including bosses) than they are to other dudes.
- When women bosses act more "masculine," men they manage are more likely to complain about being overworked than if a male boss acts the same way.

Though research is showing people are caring less and less about the gender of their bosses (a great thing), dudes with issues working for a woman are going to have a hard time. Because more women have degrees, more of them take manager roles that require skills they get in college. Women now make up 30% of corporate executive positions, and almost half of all management positions in America.

Men who want to should try to be leaders and managers ourselves. But we also need to get damn comfortable working with, and sometimes for, women.

The Left and Men: Do y'all want us anymore?

When Hillary Clinton ran for President in 2016, she had a slogan: "I'm With Her." At the end of her speech at the big Democratic convention that year, she celebrated by breaking a glass ceiling. The message was simple: Women are important, have been discriminated against for years, and I will be the president for all women.

A lot of men, though, took that as a message that she wouldn't be a leader for them. She lost men 52-41, many of them in critical midwestern swing states, and Trump won.

Clinton, as a prominent member of the Democratic Party, recently made her feelings on some men clear. Just a few weeks ago, she said, "The idea that you could turn the clock back and try to recreate a world that...was dominated by— you know, let's say it—white men of a certain persuasion, a certain religion, a certain point of view, a certain ideology— it's just doing such damage to what we should be aiming for."

I supported her campaign in 2016, even introducing her husband at a rally in front of about 1,000 people before the primary election (and then took a ton of shit from Bernie supporters). To this guy who tried to get her elected, her words hit hard. I know she wasn't talking about me, but her words reflect what many on the left think about guys that look like me.

We are a problem to solve, not people who might need help. And lots of guys don't like it.

Remember, many today believe men, not women, have the deck stacked against them. Most of these folks are on the extreme side of the political spectrum, but these ideas are seeping into mainstream thought.

I've started listening to reasonable, thoughtful dudes that are NOT part of the far right about this topic. Union members, non-profit directors, Democratic operatives, and candidates.

Here's what they are saying.

- *"I work with all of these women in liberal circles, and they do not want me around."*
- *"They don't want us to be men anymore."*
- *"I read the Democratic Party's website. What? You don't want me?" (see below)*
- *"I ran for office a few years ago. Did everything I was supposed to...worked hard, raised money, got the newspaper endorsement, everything. My opponent didn't do shit. No money, no website, no door to door, but she still won. Democrats just wanted a woman."*
- *"What do they want? For me to just disappear?"*
- *"My son just started at the University of Tennessee. I was worried about him going to Berkeley, where he would get blamed for everyone's problems."*

- *"I don't even identify as a Democrat anymore. I'll still vote for them, because what's the choice? But what are we even doing?"*
- *"All these people on the left are telling me what not to do as a guy. Well, what about some direction on what I can do?"*
- *"I teach in a college English Department. There are more lesbian professors than men."*

These individual reactions are backed up by polling. American men feel the left is more extreme than the right and identify as conservative (41%) more than they do liberal (20%) or moderate (37%). 46% of young men believe that "feminism is about favoring women over men." Only 37% disagree.

Many women have had terrible life experiences, some really, *really* shitty. Historically, the laws of our country have been slanted against females and these experiences are real and their viewpoints are absolutely valid. Because of this, when I lay out the stats for men about suicide, prison, drug use, porn, AI girlfriends, education issues, and job problems, so many women on the political left respond with eye rolls or say something like "now you know how it feels" or "grow a pair and get tougher." It's the same attitude that Hillary expressed in her recent comments.

The thing is, men ARE having real problems today and the political left is turning their backs on us in a lot of ways.

My political career started in 1998 when I won a seat on my university's Student Senate. Since working for a Democrat congressional candidate in 2002, I served as a County Commissioner, State Representative, and State Secretary of Labor; represented the Democratic party as a candidate for Congress, for the Public Regulation Commission, and for State Auditor; and was even a delegate to the Young Democrats 2003 National Convention in Buffalo.

I was proud to work on progressive stuff. I pushed for "big" issues like legalizing weed and gay marriage, raising and enforcing the minimum wage, and asking rich people to pay a bit more in taxes. I worked hard on "smaller" ones too like getting sewer systems to neighborhoods, encouraging kids to bike to school, and helping build services for people living on the street. I voted to protect women's rights over their own bodies, defended immigrants who want to come here for a better life for themselves, and carried out new laws that fought climate change.

I'm retired from politics now, though, and only tell you that to tell you this. Like some of those guys quoted above, I wonder sometimes if the left even wants me anymore?

Who the Democrats Represent

For starters? The Democratic National Committee's website. Though recently taken down, during 2024-2025 there was a page called *Who We Serve* listing all of the groups the party supposedly represents. It started by stating that "Democrats are the party of inclusion" before listing sixteen groups:

African Americans. Americans with Disabilities. Asian Americans and Pacific Islanders. Democrats Abroad. Ethnic Americans. Latinos. Faith Community. LGBTQ+ Community. Native Americans. Rural Americans. Seniors and Retirees. Small Business Community. Union Members and Families. Veterans and Military Families. Women. Young People and Students.

In other words, the Democrats represent all women, but only certain men? That's the actual message of this list. Which begs the question: **If Dems are really the party of inclusion, then why am I and men like me not included?**

When James Carville made a plea for Democrats to appeal more to men in 2024, the opposition from Dem pollster Anna Greenberg was stark. She argued that the party should solely focus on things like abortion and Republicans rolling back decades of progress for women. She also said, "Carville may not like it, but the Democratic Party *is the women's party.* Sixty percent of self-identified Democrats are women."

In the summer of 2025, I was in Washington DC talking with a staffer for a large organization focused on getting Latino folks to vote for Democrats. She said their specific focus was on reaching Latino men. I asked her how many men the organization had working on their staff. The answer? Zero.

By the way, brown men shifted their votes from Biden to Trump by 18% in the last election.

Democrats have so many organizations that focus on women. There is a National Federation of Democratic Women and a Women's National Democratic Club. Outside organizations like Emily's List and EMERGE exist to strategically recruit, educate, and fund women to run as Democrats.

Even though, as Dr Greenberg told us, the Democratic party is now majority women, there are no equivalent organizations for fellas.

To many in the party, men are a problem to be solved, not people who need representation.

'24 Presidential Race

Kamala Harris ran a good campaign, and I was happy to vote for her. But like Clinton, she lost men, only winning 43% of us. While she strategically did not take Hillary Clinton's direct approach in messaging, a lot of guys still felt left out of her campaign? Why?

First, Trump made a real effort to go to the places where guys congregate. He went on fourteen major podcasts, focusing on the ones that men listen to like comedians Joe Rogan and Andrew Shultz, sports shows like ex-professional-wrestler The Undertaker's *Six Feet Under* and Barstool Sports' *Bussin With The Boys*, and popular Youtubers The Nelk Boys and Logan Paul. He went to Ultimate Fighting Championship fights, NASCAR races, and top end college football games. Gaming streamer Adin Ross not only hosted Trump on his site, he bet $1 million on Trump winning, signaling an affinity for gambling (another thing a ton of guys like).

He talked about things men care about, too, like bringing down the price of stuff, taking away the tax on tips (more men are trending to lower wage jobs as we go to school less), and pushing tariffs to bring back jobs for dudes.

These were simple, easy things to understand, and guys heard it.

Kamala did go on a few podcasts for black men (*All the Smoke, Club Shay Shay, Charlamagne tha God*) and she talked to Howard Stern. She took on former high school football coach Tim Walz as her running mate, and he tried some of the same strategies Trump did: attending football games, pheasant hunting, and Twitch streaming games with Rep

Alexandria Ocasio Cortez.

However, she turned down an invitation for Rogan because her campaign was worried about "progressive backlash." Walz, even in his efforts, wasn't as effective in going where men, especially young ones, congregate.

Neither really talked simply about things that would help out most guys. They rolled out a strategy to help black men, but didn't address dudes of other races. Some of the other things she campaigned on, like supporting apprenticeships or helping families care for older members, were complicated and didn't break through the same way Trump's stuff did. We'll get into this later.

DEI

Diversity, equity, and inclusion (DEI) training and policies have been in the news a lot lately. It started for a very good reason. Women and minorities have been hamstrung from being able to compete for years both by laws and the fact that people tend to hire people that look like they do. Because men were almost always in charge, they would hire other men, making it hard for women to get a foot in the door even if they educated themselves, worked hard, and got shit done.

So DEI training, and policies like affirmative action, were put in place to help fight this situation by creating a more even playing field. A friend of mine works as a DEI trainer, and she tries so hard to make sure those conversations are not about blame. She brings everyone's perspective into discussions and focuses on the positive things diversity brings to any organization. There are many people like her out there.

But there are also many that aren't.

Another friend of mine is a teacher in Central Texas. He's a reasonable, forward-thinking guy who believes passionately in public education, full equality for women, and that we should do something about climate change. But over drinks one time, he was telling me about the DEI training his school district put in place right before COVID. As part of the program, to explain the concept of privilege, they had everyone stand in a part of the classroom. As a white, straight, man, he was put at the front of the class and told in front of everyone else that he had all the advantages of society while everyone else was suffering.

The implication was an attack, like it was his fault. He told me his immediate reaction was, "What the fuck did I do?"

He is not alone.

Joanne Lipman, a former corporate executive with Gannett (America's largest newspaper publisher), left the job a few years ago to write a book and become an expert on trying to reshape how DEI is talked about. Specifically, she spent three years trying to find out how to get men more involved in these workplace issues. In this work, she discovered something interesting. A ton of DEI training was about one thing: blaming men, especially white, straight ones, for problems in society.

She spoke to one DEI trainer who brutally said the whole point of DEI training was to "bang white guys over the head with a 2x4. We want them to feel guilty, and if we make them cry, all the better."

This is a shitty strategy. Frank Dobbin and Michele Lamont, professors at Harvard Business School, studied thirty years' worth of diversity training at over 800 companies. They found that for women (and black men), that type of training actually made things worse in terms of diversity at their companies. The men forced into the training felt (surprise, surprise) attacked and resentful about the whole process, and were even more inclined to hire people that looked like them.

What Today's Men See

The traditional view from the left in the last few decades has been that since men are already enmeshed in power, we don't need any recognition. Organizations and support for men aren't required, because society as a whole exists to give us success. Views like this drive the kind of thinking that populates the Dem Party's website. Historically it's been an accurate worldview.

Men today though, *especially young ones*, see it differently. And they have a point.

Education

- A ton of organizations exist to help girls get through middle and high school. Girls, Inc, the Girls Rule Foundation, TechGirlz, Young Enterprising Women, and Awesome Math Girls are only the tip of the iceberg.
- Roughly 75% of teachers in U.S. public schools are women, so may never see a male teacher in the classroom. But boys need male role models to succeed.
- There are 4x more college scholarships available to women than men.
- There are 276 degree programs for Women's and

Gender Studies at U.S. colleges with no equivalent organizations for dudes.
- Many schools have double digit professional and academic organizations to support women. Organizations to give guys the same kind of help don't exist.

So what do many boys see?

They see that last year, girls made up 70% of high school valedictorians. They graduate at higher rates from high school than we do and they are getting into college and completing their degrees at an almost 2-to-1 rate.

So they have an advantage at all levels of school. Why, then are they still getting all the help while dudes get none? To many, it doesn't feel fair.

Jobs/Housing

- Government programs exist to help women get into "non-traditional jobs." There aren't any for men.
- There are almost 2,000 professional organizations that exist to help women succeed at work, with no equivalent for men.
- Organizations to educate women about home ownership and construction/maintenance exist. Some states even market programs specifically to help with housing for single moms, but single dads are never mentioned.

What do guys see? Young male professionals are out of work more than women of the same age, the gender wage gap has basically disappeared for people aged 25-34, and young women are buying more than double the houses than young men are.

So they see women doing better at jobs, making more money, and buying more houses. Why then are they getting all the support while men get none? That doesn't seem right.

And young men today see their brothers are way more likely to be in prison, kill ourselves, be addicted to hard drugs, and get fatter than women. Yet 75% of mental health counselors are women, when many dudes prefer and are more open with male therapists.

Many guys are hurting, don't have places to gather, and think no one cares.

These are the things that give people like Tucker Carlson the ammunition to say, "American men are in deep trouble," and that we are "pretty close to being destroyed." And men are listening.

Two Things at Once

I DO NOT agree with Carlson, nor do I think the Democratic Party should stop supporting things like abortion, prosecution of sexual harassment/assault, child support, or the like. I worry deeply about the future of women in this country, and know we do have the responsibility to build a country where everyone has an equal shot at success.

But we have to walk and chew gum at the same time.

If people teaching DEI want to actually be successful, they have to bring men into the conversation and not just try to make us cry. Dems need to promote issues important to women while taking the real problems men face seriously.

Men ARE people who deserve representation and help. We aren't just problems to be solved.

The left is supposed to stand for inclusion, good government, and a Constitution for all people, right? To do that we have to bring everyone to the table. It's not only the right thing to do...if we don't, we will probably keep losing.

CHAPTER 23

Losing Men is
Losing Political Strategy

Many men are turning away from the political left and the Democratic party. This has real consequences for those of us who want a more progressive future. Let's really understand what this will mean for the future of our communities if the trend continues.

Losing Men Is a Losing Strategy

Since 2016, white men under thirty moved roughly 17 points toward the GOP in their voting while younger non-white men moved more than 30 points. Hispanic men moved 18 points from Biden in 2020 to Trump in 2024. This is the first time a Republican got the majority of the brown male vote in years. And even though the only, true male focus the Harris campaign had was for black men, she actually lost their votes compared to 2020. Biden got 87% of black males in 2020. Harris only got 75% of them.

Interestingly enough, even though Harris strategically

didn't use the same "break the glass ceiling" approach Hillary Clinton campaigned on in 2016, she actually lost men by a point more than Hillary did.

As we saw in 2024, this obviously does not make for a winning presidential campaign. It can hurt down the ballot as well. As Americans sort themselves by political ideology, moving to places where they feel more comfortable, it gives right wing candidates a constant advantage both in the Electoral College (where Trump's 2016 victory happened even though he lost the popular vote) and in the U.S. Senate.

Why? Every state gets two senators, no matter how many people they have. So in these elections one vote in Wyoming (population 584,000) gets the same influence as 68 votes in California (population 39.5 million) for one-sixth of the entire federal government. Furthermore, since the electoral college is a combination of the House of Representatives (an accurate measure of the populations' opinion overall) and the Senate, it tilts voting weight in Presidential elections towards rural voters. Rural voters are now consistently and overwhelmingly Republican.

While Harris and Democrats did OK with urban, more highly educated men, losing working class men hurts the left in rural states where these guys' votes have more influence. This hamstrings Dems' ability to compete in future senate and presidential contests.

It's an issue moving forward as well. Popular presidents tend to influence how younger people living during their presidential terms vote as they get older. Trump has maintained his popularity among many men, even winning re-election after a loss, which suggests people in 2024 still trusted him.

So many of these young guys that are turning right might be more inclined to stay that way throughout their lives.

Ignoring Men Doesn't Lose Just Male Votes

The other political domino in this discussion isn't actually men at all. We've discussed in detail how the political right is using their power to screw women, from making abortion illegal to signaling that rape is OK. But a lot of women still voted for Trump, and one of the biggest reasons is fear for their sons' futures.

Every man out there has two birth parents, and one of them is a woman. In the three presidential elections since 2016, Democrats have won a smaller share of women's votes every year, going from winning them by 15 points in 2016 to only 7 points in 2024. Trump actually won white women in 2024 by 4 points, 2 points more than he won them in 2016 over Hillary.

Now, some would argue that people are latently both sexist AND racist, and that hurt Harris more than Clinton. But even if true it wasn't what people said their concerns were, and we should take people at their word. That idea also doesn't explain Haris's loss of black and brown women voters.

What does? Anxiety about their families.

46% of mothers report feeling "extremely" or "very" worried that their child might struggle with anxiety or depression. Nearly 50% of parents admit supporting their adult children because of problems affording food and housing, and 25% worry that this support will have to continue because of concern over "their children's future economic opportunities, particularly in regard to housing affordability, as well education costs and outcomes."

As we've documented extensively in this project, young men are more likely than young women to live with their parents, leave school earlier, and kill themselves while being less likely to report having friends. Obviously, then, so much of this anxiety mothers face is about the welfare of their sons. This has political consequences, because a party not taking young men's problems seriously isn't listening to their mothers either.

In 2016, one of the main reasons 62% of white women without college degrees voted for Trump was fear and frustration over "diminished possibilities for their husbands and sons to provide for their families." A Gen X woman who voted for Trump in 2024 was more blunt. "I'm trying to send my son to college next year, and I trust conservative policies more than liberal ones to improve my family's finances."

If the left and Democrats can do more to help young men and boys, without taking away efforts to continue empowering women, it will help more men AND women be comfortable voting for candidates.

Lastly, but importantly, this doesn't mean the left has to put up only dude candidates. There is no polling evidence showing that men won't support a woman. Gretchen Whitmer won 51% of men in her last re-election for Michigan governor. Young men supported both female candidates for 2025 Governor races in New Jersey and Virginia. Polling even shows young men give a net +18 favorability rating to Alexandria Ocasio-Cortez.

Those female candidates took men seriously. And won. How? Let's take a look.

CHAPTER 24

Walk and Chew Gum at the Same Time

Now that we know the real, hard political consequences of losing men we should also realize dudes aren't lost forever. Guys will vote for the people we can relate to and that will help us out in real ways. It's actually not that hard, and starts with admitting that men are people that need representation. After that, politicians can address problems men face in real ways.

Acknowledge the Problem

Polling after the 2024 election found that many young American men feel like they are "invisible to the Democratic coalition." An attendee to the Democratic Convention in 2024 has a son who feels "Democrats don't speak to men." Another assessment finds that "Democrats have become the party of college-educated voters" which becomes a gender issue because, as we've covered extensively, women are going to college and fellas are not.

53% of young men feel that Democrats are the better party for promoting the issues of trans people, versus 11% for the Republicans. 42% believe Democrats are the better party for promoting the interests of women, versus 17% for Republicans.

Only 18% feel like Democrats are the better party for promoting the interests of men, *versus 39% for Republicans.*

Richard Reeves, who wrote *Of Boys and Men*, and heads the American Institute for Boys and Men, recaps the last election from a gender perspective. "I think a lot of young men had the sense that the Democrats didn't see them as having problems. They saw them as being the problem. There was also a tone deafness to [the Democrats] trying to browbeat men into voting for them. Some of the language was more about, 'If you care about women, you'll vote for us.' Frank Luntz did a focus group of men and found that this messaging drove men more securely into the Republican column. As did the claims that the only reason men might not be voting the right way was because of sexism. That really backfired."

Former Transportation Secretary and Presidential candidate Pete Buttegeig took on the issue as well in a recent GQ interview. "I think for a lot of people, they would only expect the left to use the word masculinity after the word toxic. And so the bottom fell out of any kind of alternative account of what *masculinity* is or ought to be, which of course is something I think my side very much has a responsibility to put forward, instead of just always seeming to be against them."

Reeves agrees with Buttegeig, rejecting the idea that feminism has gone too far, and that "paying more attention to boys and men does not mean backing off the cause of women...A world of floundering men will not be one of flourishing women, or vice versa."

So, for starters, the left needs to simply acknowledge the issues American men are facing. The DNC can update their website to include men (including guys like me). Political candidates can openly talk about the problems men are having, and say simple things like, "We're here for you, too."

It's not that hard, and doesn't take anything away from the important work in advocating for women. We can, and should, be on the side of everyone.

Go Where the Guys Are

The left cannot be scared to actively go where guys are, meet them where they're at, and listen to their concerns. You can pay all the pollsters you want, but if people don't trust you, they are not going to support you. And they won't trust you if you don't talk to them. As Dem strategist Ross Morales Rocketto accurately points out, "The Democratic Party is missing that we're not going to be able to message our way out of these deep problems men are facing, starting with the fact that they know the Democratic Party doesn't really like or respect them."

Luckily, this isn't a hard thing to fix, as there are some really easy places to start.

Podcasts: Men are getting their news and attention from podcasts and popular online streams. There's nothing stopping people in the center and on the left from going there. It should have been a no-brainer for Kamala Harris to go on *Call Her Daddy* (the #1 Spotify podcast for women) AND *The Joe Rogan Experience*. James Talarico, a Democrat Texas

State Rep and candidate for U.S. Senate, went on Rogan in 2025 and did well. Scott Galloway, not a candidate but another passionate advocate for reasonable policies to help young men, went on Theo Vaugn's podcast last year to talk about the need for positive role models in men's lives.

These podcasts are not enemy territory. Hosts want intelligent, deep discussions about what is going on in the world around them. Some may have differing views than the public officials or experts going on their platforms, but many value honesty and authenticity. And, as Buttigieg pointed out about his frequent appearances on Fox News, it is critical to "find out where there's a lot of people who don't agree with you and get in there and take your shot."

Unions: A traditional support group for the left, unions are made up of an overwhelmingly male membership. But now 40% of all union members consider themselves Republican, with many feeling that Trump talked more directly to the problems of working class people. Recently, a business manager for a trades union in Dallas told me his membership was 50/50. Many see the left as taking them for granted and viewing Democrat attitudes toward men as...not great. The best example is the Teamsters. They refused to endorse Harris in 2024, the first time that a major union didn't endorse a Dem candidate for President since 1996.

They would, however, welcome people going to their meetings, deeply listening to their members, and understanding their issues. This would include things like better wages, more construction jobs, and addressing mental health concerns. The Plumbers and Pipefitters, Laborers, Sheet Metal Workers, and others all are now establishing programs to take the issue of mental health head-on as the construction and mining trades have the highest rate of suicide for any American employment area.

Sports: Football is America's most popular sport by far. 41% of Americans say it is their favorite, with basketball (10%) and baseball (9%) far behind. The Army-Navy game is one of football's biggest traditions. Played since 1890, it is always set on a weekend in December after other college football championship games, becoming America's de facto college game of that week every year. It also celebrates the young people studying to become officers in two of our military branches. Trump goes to every game as President.

Joe Biden never attended during his term. Neither did Kamala Harris.

Sports podcasts and internet content trail only gaming forums and comedy for the attention of young men. For politicians, showing that you have a shared interest is a way to establish connection. Barack Obama famously made his NCAA tournament bracket pick public every year, and still does. George W. Bush brought the country together after 9/11 by throwing out the first pitch at Yankees Stadium in Game 3 of the World Series, getting a massive cheer when he threw a perfect strike. Bill Clinton sat courtside to watch his home state Arkansas Razorbacks in the 1994 NCAA tournament, and Ronald Reagan did an interview before the 1987 Fiesta Bowl talking about his history as a sportscaster.

Some Democrats get this. In 2025, U.S. Senator Mark Kelly and House Minority Leader Hakeem Jeffries did interviews on one of sports' most watched podcasts, *The Dan LeBatard Show.* Kelly talked about the government shutdown, his experiences as an astronaut, and his thoughts on the Arizona Cardinals not having the greatest of seasons. Jeffries went in depth on the New York Knicks' bench rotation strategy, while also talking about health care issues and the evolving conflict with Venezuela.

Other left-leaning politicians should do the same.

Policies

Public policy can be super complicated. The trick, though, is to tell people in simple terms what it means for them. The left in general can be pretty bad at this, insisting on giving voters a masters' thesis full of complicated words describing things rather than what they have the bandwidth to understand.

Let's take one of Kamala Harris' policy rollouts for the 2024 election: her proposals to help black men. In addition to coming out in favor of legalized marijuana, she wrote about establishing a National Health Equity Initiative, forgivable business loans for black entrepreneurs, and a regulatory framework for cryptocurrency.

These all seem good, but I went to fucking Harvard and even I don't know what a National Health Equity Initiative actually means.

Donald Trump has won the messaging war against the left, most especially with men, by simplifying what he wants to do. Things like "Build The Wall" and "No Tax On Tips" are easy to say, easy to understand, and an effective way to connect people with issues they care about (in this case, immigration and the economy).

This shouldn't be too hard to fix either. Here are a few things the left can talk about:

Build More Fucking Houses. Polls show that for young men, "owning a home is important to me" is the highest response for defining "the good life." Remember, 52% of young men still live with their parents and 23% of male renters say they had to "take on a side hustle or other job" to afford rent.

Things like removing outdated zoning rules and using public land for housing will make more affordable homes and apartments available for guys; an easy thing to communicate at the local, state, and national levels. Banning junk fees (things like "convenience charges," mandatory utility fees, and common area maintenance) would also lower the cost of an apartment, and is something every renter can relate to.

More Roads, Bridges, Trains, Airports, Solar Panels, Windmills, and Internet. We need all of these things in America, and dudes get most of the construction work the projects require. The U.S., though, is slower than other countries in getting these things done. We need to get rid of the red tape unnecessarily holding most of these projects up and get them done faster. It's a win-win; both good for our society and men working in the trades.

Speaking of which...

Get Your Ass Through School. Men who voted for Harris AND Trump both believe that "fulfilling jobs," "having enough money to do what you want to do," and "financial independence" are important to their ideas of success. Guys may not be going to traditional college, but they are heading to community college and apprentice classes to learn trades leading to good jobs once they get their degree or certificate.

This is great *if they finish their education.*

The yearly retention rate for men at community college is only 52% while only about 50-60% of apprentices (who are 80% dudes) complete their certificates. Democrats can listen to these guys, find out why they're not finishing, (timing flexibility, money for tools, etc.), and build support for those areas so they can go make that bag.

More Male Teachers. Boys perform better and respond better to dude teachers. Only about 25% of teachers, though, are men. Getting more fellas in the classroom provides them stable jobs in areas that AI will have a hard time replacing, and helps students by providing a balanced educational experience. Harris' plan for black men talked about "strengthening the Public Service Loan Forgiveness Program to recruit more black men for the classroom."

It's a really good idea, so why not say it with less...multi-syllable words? "Bro, we need you teaching. Get your education degree and a job in the schools. Then we'll pay off your student loans. Deal?"

We could also consider something similar for nurses, social workers, and mental health professionals. All are areas where we need more people, and especially more men.

Some on the left are actually getting this shit.

- California Gov Gavin Newsom recently put out an Executive Order to increase attention for male mental health, work, and education issues.
- Connecticut Gov Ned Lamont talked about increasing male teachers in his 2025 State of the State address.
- Michigan Gov Gretchen Whitmer wants more men in higher education and skills training.
- Maryland Gov Wes Moore has just started initiatives to get more men into education and healthcare.
- In 2026, the Virginia legislature passed a bill creating a Commission on Men and Boys. Signed by Gov Abigail Spanberger, the goal is finding better policies on health care, education, jobs, and social media.

These are all great initiatives! Now the hard work comes into play by putting meat on the bone in accomplishable, understandable ways.

Strength and Government That Works

American men don't feel like things today are working for them. They see governments and schools as failures and bleak prospects for housing, jobs, and a family. Many young people of both sexes don't put real importance on voting, and a recent global poll showed that 27% of U.S. young people would prefer having a king to a democracy. 23% didn't care, and only 40% said it would be actually bad.

This is not great.

Men see other powerful guys like Jeff Bezos with

Amazon, Elon Musk with Tesla and Starlink, and Steve Jobs with Apple, as strong leaders who built things that work (well, not you, Cybertruck).

Trump appealed to this need for strength directly. He called himself a "warrior," a "protector," and described the election as a "battle." He surrounded himself with big guys like wrestler Hulk Hogan, UFC owner Dana White, and ex-NFL running back Hershel Walker. He talked glowingly about the size of Arnold Palmer's cock.

Look, this strategy has issues. But the result is that more men saw a guy who was not going to fuck around, one who would blow up the current system that they hate. A person authentic enough to say what he wanted, when he wanted to, and not worry about what people in that system thought. A guy who was strong enough to change the world around us, because even if he is a bad person, what could be worse than now?

34% of young men view Republicans as "strong." Only 18% feel that way about Democrats.

But it doesn't have to be that way.

We can be strong enough to speak our minds, not worrying about what every pollster says about every word. Hell, we can even fucking curse once in a while.

Like Talarico and Buttigieg, we can be strong enough to go to where people are, even those we may disagree with. Listening to their real stories and shooting our shot with good ideas is a show of confidence and toughness.

We can be strong enough to get shit done. When the Philadelphia I-95 bridge collapsed in 2023, Gov Josh Shapiro got it rebuilt in twelve days. New York Mayor Zoran Mamdani announced progress after 100 days in office that included paving over 100,000 potholes. That is strength and leadership that we can do more of.

We can be strong enough to show compassion and understanding for the women who have been raped, discriminated against, interrupted constantly, denied positions and promotion because of their gender while pushing for things like universal child care and against efforts to take away their healthcare, right to vote, or ability to get a divorce.

We can ALSO be strong enough to also show compassion and understanding for the men who feel alone, afraid, and unsupported enough to withdraw into the internet and eventually shoot up a school, or themselves, while pushing for things like more role models, good jobs, and housing.

This is what real strength is. The left can do this just as easily as Trump. And we can do it in a way that will actually make things better.

So what the hell are we waiting for?

Dudes, Christianity, and Nationalism

I recently started working out at the New Mexico State University Activities Center gym, the same one I used as a student in the late '90s. The first day when I got in at 6:30 a.m., there was a student asleep at the front desk and I realized that some things never change.

One big change, though? Compared to my student days, there are so many more men in the gym wearing large and visible crosses, sporting shirts with Christian themes like "Forgiven" and "Aggies For Life" (NMSU has the same mascot as Texas A&M), and showing off large Christian tattoos. The ladies? Every once in a while, I see one with a small cross necklace, but they are much rarer.

The Situation

It turns out, I am not imagining things.

Women traditionally go to church more than men, but that's changing. Guys around fifty years old are the least likely to attend church on a regular basis. Dudes born after 2000, though, go to church a lot more.

Young men are also reportedly reading the Bible more, and say they are much more "committed to Jesus" than their older brothers. The reasoning is very consistent with all of the research documented in this project. "Gen Z men are reporting higher levels of disconnection, isolation, and uncertainty about their futures. Many struggle with dating, forming friendships, or finding stable paths toward adulthood. For some, the church offers a sense of stability, belonging, and clarity that's difficult to find elsewhere."

A young Gen Z woman on the "Explain It to Me" podcast puts it bluntly, "The Church is one of the only places that lets men be men."

Furthermore, young men are choosing churches that lean right and "traditional." There has been a resurgence in attendance at Latin Catholic mass. Dwight Longenecker, right-wing priest from South Carolina argues that's because old school churches subscribe to a "mendicant life" that favors "large families, classical schools and dynamic orthodoxy" and rejects the "rainbow politics and ideologies that have poisoned and weakened so much of the Catholic Church over the last thirty years."

Some say these masses, along with evangelical churches that have similar traditions, give men a place where fellow men lead a consistent, traditional ceremony with repetitive rituals. This gives a sense of solidity in a quickly-changing world. A darker view is that they are attracted to a message of "how great they really are and promise a return to rigid, traditional gender hierarchies that benefit them."

Young women, on the other hand, are going in the other

direction. More Gen Z women than men are leaving the religion they were brought up in, as a vast majority identify as feminist and "don't believe that churches treat men and women equally." Many rate improving their professional lives far higher than having a family, something churches generally emphasize, and most conservative religions specifically forbid women from real leadership positions.

This "stained glass ceiling" rubs a lot of women the wrong way.

The idea that men want a place that makes them feel included in a world they see as ignoring them is more about identity and less about how one views their relationship with God. And a bunch of people want to take advantage of that for political purposes.

Their name? Christian Nationalists.

Religion and America

When European settlers first started coming over to what became the USA, they were in the middle of a 200-year stretch where Christians were murdering each other. The most deaths came during the Thirty Years War between Lutherans and Catholics in Germany, Sweden, Holland, France, and Spain. *One-third of the German population died.* There were also British Civil Wars, a Swiss Civil War, and Protestant rebellions in France against the Catholic nobility. The Spanish Inquisition killed between 3,000-5,000 Jews, Muslims, and Protestants for not being Catholic enough, mostly by burning them at the stake.

Millions died as people set up governments enforcing their own specific view of Christianity with prison, torture, and death.

The Pilgrims who landed in Massachusetts, the ones from our Thanksgiving stories, were made up of English Protestants who first tried moving to Holland before shipping across to North America. Their goal was a community with very conservative religious practices not allowed by the Church of England, and economic conditions in Holland had their leaders worried their followers would assimilate to the more conventional spiritual practices there.

A bigger group, calling themselves Puritans because they wanted a "purer" version of Protestant Christianity, came to North America after losing some of those British Civil Wars. They wanted a government that told people what to do, with moral standards and "true religious worship" according to their version of Christianity. Think mandatory church attendance, bans on dancing, hanging witches... that sort of thing.

Eventually, as more people who thought differently came over, things mellowed out. Rhode Island was founded by people kicked out of Massachusetts for not being strict enough, Maryland became a safe haven for Catholics, and Pennsylvania was set up for Quakers, a Christian denomination focused on peace, service, and equality of the sexes.

The dudes who wrote the Constitution separated church and state for two big reasons. First, they knew all about the European religious wars and wanted none of that shit here. Second, they seriously cared about individual liberty and didn't want governments telling people how they should talk to God.

- George Washington, the first President, asked for tolerance of everyone's spirituality in his farewell address.
- The second President, John Adams, signed a treaty stating that "The Government of the United States is not, in any sense, founded on the Christian religion."
- Thomas Jefferson and James Madison, the third and fourth Presidents, fought any government supported religion because churches supported by taxes screwed with people's individual freedom.
- Benjamin Franklin, the dude on the $100 bill, was adamant that religions should not be entangled with the government, seeing religious differences as a threat to the nation.

So when you hear people saying that we are a "Christian Nation," it's good to remember all of this.

Modern Christian Nationalism

There are a ton of people, mostly dudes, who want to turn the country into what the Puritans originally wanted: a government that enforces their religious views on everyone, whether people want it or not. This isn't about Jesus or the Bible, which we'll get into next chapter. It's about power. Examples are everywhere.

In his book, *The Case For Christian Nationalism*, Stephen Wolfe describes the ideal Christian Nationalist society. He argues that the U.S. needs to choose "similar people over dissimilar people," that "one ought to prefer and to love more those who are more similar to him," "nations have a right of exclusion in the interest of cultural preservation," and "nothing can be more fatal to mankind or to religion itself than to call one set of things or persons religious and another secular, when Christ has redeemed the whole."

What does this mean in plain English? To Wolfe and other Christian Nationalists, governments should enforce Christian morals for people *that look and think like them*. If you don't? Fuck you, get out of here. Because if America truly becomes an "official" Christian nation, rulers will use their religious opinion rather than things like democratic process or basic rights as a guidebook to do whatever they want.

An example of this is the "Great Replacement Theory," where white Christians are terrified of brown and black immigrants replacing them as the majority. Again, this isn't a new concept. In the 1800s, New York street wars were fought by "Native" Protestant Americans against Irish Catholic immigrants because they didn't want to become a city infected with Catholicism. If you've ever seen the film *Gangs of New York*, those scenes with the gang fights between Leonardo DiCaprio and Daniel Day Lewis were based on actual events.

More recently, Christian Nationalist and former Fox News pundit Tucker Carlson argues that immigration should focus on race, saying that "the Democratic Party is trying to replace the current electorate, the voters now casting ballots, with new people, more obedient voters from the Third World."

Unfortunately, this bullshit rhetoric leads to actual deaths. The recent mass murders at a synagogue in Pittsburg and a Walmart in El Paso were because shooters, both men deep in the manosphere, feared that Jews wanted "to bring invaders in that kill our people," and that immigration was leading to a "Hispanic invasion of Texas."

The next step of Christian Nationalists is to combine blind patriotism with government authority. Again, the goal isn't about spreading the word of Jesus. It's about control. Examples are everywhere. Making schools put the Ten Commandments in classrooms, like Texas, Oklahoma, and Louisiana recently did, or the new Alabama law requiring a Judeo Christian prayer right after the Pledge of Allegiance purposefully combine religious symbols with government-required education. These sort of policies pledge to do one thing: show kids that obedience to the government is holy.

What Does This Have To Do With Men?

So what does all of this Christian Nationalist stuff have to do with guys? Plenty. The book *Taking America Back for God: Christian Nationalism in the United States* by Andrew Whitehead and Samuel Perry details how a "masculine" Christianity is being embraced by the far right with a real focus on everybody staying in their "proper" place.

One of the most famous books written about a future America ruled by Christian Nationalists is called *The Handmaid's Tale*. In it, and in a more recent television adaptation, most women aren't able to have babies because of environmental issues. A group of powerful guys with a strict interpretation of the Bible take over the country, setting up the "Republic of Gilead" and ruling through a "Committee." Under this government, most women can't get an education and are only allowed to do work in the house or raise kids. Their titles include things like Wives,

Aunts, Marthas, and Jezebels.

The women who are able to bear children, but who are believed to have sinned in some way, are called Handmaids. They are assigned to dudes who rape them until they get pregnant.

If you think this is just some crazy fictional fantasy, think again, because a ton of guys in power are actively working to make this happen.

Let's start with the whole "Wives Submit To Husbands" thing. Mentioned once in the Bible (Ephesians, 5:22-24), this is a popular line among conservatives who want to limit women to only having "traditional" family roles.

The former Governor of Arkansas and current U.S Ambassador to Israel, Mike Huckabee, signed a letter in 1998 supporting the Baptist Church's position that "wives should graciously submit to their husbands." I wonder if he thinks his daughter Sarah, the current Governor of Arkansas, should do whatever her husband tells her?

Donald Trump created a White House "Office of Faith" this year (Gilead-ish right there) and appointed a woman named Paula White-Cain to run it. She says that men are the "bedrock, as God intended" and that in marriage, "If there's ever a time that a decision has to be made and we don't agree on something, he's the head. It's not hard to submit."

Charlie Kirk famously told Taylor Swift to "submit to your husband" when she got engaged to Chiefs' tight end Travis Kelce. He was so influential in the Christian Nationalist movement that President Donald Trump spoke at his funeral, and Vice President JD Vance was a pallbearer.

Next? Voting. Jesse Sumpter, an influential Christian

pastor, authored an article, "Husband, Make Sure Your Wife Votes Exactly Like You Do." In it, he argues that the Bible calls for husbands to have complete control of their wives' bodies. He, therefore, should control her vote.

His older brother Toby Sumpter, another powerful preacher, goes farther, calling voting a "holy sacrament" (again, combining government and religion) where only the head of the household, the husband, should vote.

Before you think these are just a bunch of crazy nutjobs who don't have real influence in anything, Toby's interview on CNN espousing this crap was praised and re-posted by the Secretary of Defense, Pete Hegseth. In addition, Newt Gingrich, former Republican Speaker of the House of Representatives, said a wife not telling her husband how she voted is "corrupt." In response to a Democratic ad in the 2024 race in which a woman lies to her husband about her vote, Trump responded with the following, "But the wives and husbands, I don't think that's the way they deal. I mean, can you imagine a wife not telling her husband who she's voting for? You ever hear anything like that? Even if you have a horrible—if you had a bad relationship, you're gonna tell your husband. It's a ridiculous ad, it's so stupid."

Hegseth, by the way, openly displays Christian Nationalist tattoos.

The scariest part about all of this, and the one most like the world of *The Handmaid's Tale*, is how Vice President JD Vance feels. According to Vance, women are only happy when they are married with kids. He thinks divorce is "too easy," women in violent marriages shouldn't get divorced, and raped women who get pregnant should always have to give birth to their rapist's child. Apparently to him rape is just "inconvenient." And he believes that the "whole purpose" of a woman who is too old to have kids is to help raise grandchildren.

One of Vance's biggest backers, billionaire founder of PayPal and Facebook board member Peter Thiel, literally sees *The Handmaid's Tale* not as a warning, but as a goals document. He's said women voting is one of the biggest reasons we can't be "optimistic about politics." He wrote an essay saying, "I no longer believe freedom and democracy are compatible." He also said in a book that, "Monarchy is the best form of government." This guy spoke at the 2016 Republican National Convention and gave Vance over $16 million when he ran for the U.S. Senate.

Other tech dudes who support Vance? Software developer Curtis Yarvin, who wants a dictator in charge of America, and ultra-Catholic Notre Dame professor Patrick Deneen. Deneen's book is called *Regime Change* and calls for a military takeover of the U.S. government to enforce his view of religious law. Vance openly asked Donald Trump to do what Yarvin wants, and appeared with Deneen at a book signing.

These guys worked for years to get a Supreme Court majority that would make abortion illegal again. They got it, and now because one-third of U.S. women don't have access to abortion, some are bleeding to death in parking lots because doctors are too scared to help them. In addition, three states have active proposals to remove a woman's right to a divorce should she just be unhappy with her marriage. And, in Vance's home state of Ohio, a proposal to limit common types of contraception for women was introduced in 2025.

This Doesn't Help

Fellas, none of this helps us. These guys that want to take over? They don't care about getting you a good job, helping you get through school (whatever that looks like), or building affordable places to live. They just want more money, more power, and to use your need for community, connection, and structure to get it.

If going to church makes you feel some connection to God and helps you with your spiritual path, that can be super healthy. In doing this, though, I only have two requests.

First, if your religious leaders start advocating for this government stuff, recognize exactly what they want and why.

Second, please read the actual words of Jesus Christ in the Gospels...which we'll talk about next.

CHAPTER 26

What Would Jesus (Really) Do?

My dad came from an Irish Catholic family. He was an altar boy as a kid and went to religious school from kindergarten through his degree at the University of Dayton in Ohio, a Marianist Catholic college. He cared a lot about my family's faith, so my sister and I started out at Catholic school and went to Mass every Sunday through our teenage years.

But it wasn't really my thing. Though some people love the ritual and consistency of a Catholic Mass, it just never really spoke to me. The best church experiences I ever had were at Mt. Zion Baptist Church in Austin, Texas. It was in my neighborhood, had amazing music, and a positive, energetic vibe that left me smiling every time I went. Rev

Daryl Horton gave these smart, energetic, uplifting, forty-five-minute sermons about community that made me feel better every time I attended.

Being one of the only white people in there, it could have been weird. It wasn't. Everyone was super welcoming and supportive.

Look, everyone can have a different way to get spiritual fulfillment. My grandmother loved the solidity, tradition, and comfort of Catholic Mass. I got into the energy, music, and positivity of a Black Baptist Church. Other people may find their way through Judaism, Islam, Buddhism, or simply by witnessing the connection of everything while walking through nature. It's your choice, and I hope everyone has the opportunity to find a vehicle to spiritual fulfillment that works for them.

With some forms of Christianity, though, I get confused sometimes. We know more dudes are going back to traditional Catholic and Evangelical churches for the community, structure, and leadership they feel it provides. However, once they go, they end up listening to leaders who preach twisted values about things like money, gay folks, women, and the like.

Look, I'm no biblical scholar. But I do know how to read, so a few years ago, I went through the Gospels again for the first time since middle school Catholic class. These are the four books in the Bible describing the final three years of Jesus' life, from when he began preaching to when he was crucified. I wanted to take a fresh look at where Jesus was coming from, and two thoughts came to my mind after I got done:

1. "This Jesus guy is awesome and honestly kind of a bad ass."
2. "Did these 'Christian' dudes read the book about the guy they named themselves after? Because what Jesus says and what these guys do doesn't seem to jive."

There are a ton of examples of this disconnect.

Money and The Rich

Joel Osteen is a really popular Christian preacher. Over 50,000 people attend his weekly services in the old Houston Rockets basketball stadium. He's sold over twenty million books, has three million YouTube subscribers, and his church claims his TV show is viewed by "twenty million people each month in almost 100 countries around the world."

He is also very, very rich. His net worth is in the range of $100 million, his mansion in Houston is worth over $10 million, and he flies around in a private jet his church owns. Osteen is proud of his money, and talks about a thing called the prosperity gospel: "God wants us to prosper financially, to have plenty of money, to fulfill the destiny He has laid out for us."

Basically, he defends his money with a simple mantra. If God wants me to be rich, who am I to argue?

Another extremely wealthy guy who talks about his Christian faith? Donald Trump. He proudly calls his favorite book the Bible (selling his version for millions of dollars), and in his 2025 inaugural address said he was "saved by God to make America great again."

In case you've been living under a rock since the '80s, Trump likes to show off his wealth and hang out with other extremely rich people. Like Osteen, he flies around in his own private plane. He decked out his New York apartment completely in gold. Memberships to his Florida resort sell for $1 million a pop.

Here is the funny thing though. Jesus? Over and over again, he railed about how insane amounts of wealth are bad.

Three of the Gospels describe Jesus having a conversation with this young rich guy who asks about getting to heaven. After telling him to not lie, cheat, steal, or murder, the dude responds that he's got all this down and asks what more he can do. Jesus tells him straight up, "If you want to be perfect, go, sell your possessions and give to the poor, and you will have treasure in heaven. Then come, follow me." The rich guy got super sad and walked away because he obviously liked his bankroll. After that, Jesus tells his followers, "*It is easier for a camel to go through the eye of a needle than for someone who is rich to enter the kingdom of God.*"

Camels are big. Needles are not. The metaphor is pretty obvious.

In another story, Jesus found some bankers and animal merchants in a temple, trying to make money off the worshippers. So he storms in there and flips all of their tables, spills their shit, and tells them to stop making money in a place of worship.

When I hear about Trump Bibles, then remember this story, it seems pretty obvious Trump didn't read the thing he is selling.

In other parts of the Bible, Jesus says if you love money,

you cannot serve God, called a guy who hoarded tons of wealth a fool, and said people who only want money can't get any spiritual comfort. Jesus' message is consistent, clear, and passionate.

Look, working hard with a goal of living a comfortable life is something I think everyone can get behind. No one is saying we shouldn't pay our bills. But Jesus raises serious questions about those who claim to be super Christians and then tell you their main goal is to be super rich.

The Sick and Hungry

A lot of folks on the political right, the same guys working to recruit dudes openly wearing crosses, seem to get off on screwing over poor people. The most modern example? In the summer of 2025, Trump and Republicans in Congress passed a budget that mercilessly cut food for the hungry and financial help for sick people going to the doctor. Rural hospitals started closing immediately. Meanwhile, they cut taxes for the super rich.

We can and should have conversations about the role of government in helping the less fortunate people in our society. That kind of debate is one of the things that makes America beautiful.

But Trump and Congress? They slashed help with glee and snark. Trump said it gets "America winning again." Conservative Christian and Speaker of the House Mike Johnson called it a "huge victory."

Iowa Senate Republican Jonie Earnst *literally joked about killing people.* When a concerned constituent asked about deaths increasing because people couldn't see a doctor, she simply replied, "We are all going to die." She doubled down a couple of days later with a sarcastic video from a graveyard, comparing people worried about more deaths for the poor with belief in the tooth fairy.

The fucking tooth fairy.

Jesus, though, does not screw around in his lessons on how we should treat the poor and sick. One of the Bible's biggest miracles? Jesus fed 5,000 people from a basket that had only five pieces of bread and a couple of fish. He healed a blind dude and cured a leper, a nasty disease caused by a bacteria that can make your nose fall off, rot your skin, and leave you so weak you can't walk.

He instructed all of us to treat our neighbors with the same kind of care. The most famous example of this is the parable of the Sheep and Goats from the book of Matthew:

Then the King will say to those on his right, 'Come, you who are blessed by my Father; take your inheritance, the kingdom prepared for you since the creation of the world. For I was hungry and you gave me something to eat, I was thirsty and you gave me something to drink, I was a stranger and you invited me in, I needed clothes and you clothed me, I was sick and you looked after me, I was in prison and you came to visit me.'

"Then the righteous will answer him, 'Lord, when did we see you hungry and feed you, or thirsty and give you something to drink? When did we see you a stranger and invite you in, or needing clothes and clothe you? When did we see you sick or in prison and go to visit you?'

*"The King will reply, '**Truly I tell you, whatever you did for one of the least of these brothers and sisters of mine, you did for me.**'*

The message here is crystal clear. People who want to really live up to Jesus' standards shouldn't let other people starve or sick people go without care. Celebrating others' suffering goes completely against Jesus' direction.

Immigration

The Christian Nationalists we described believe that society can only function well when you live around people that look like you. This has progressed into a zeal for "protecting the border," which now has the U.S. government using military forces to track down brown people (including American citizens), put them in jail, torture them, and export them to foreign torture dungeons.

These guys claim to be Christian, but Jesus was pretty direct about how we should treat people whether they look like us or not. It didn't stop with the story above that says inviting a stranger in is the right thing to do.

He told a story once about this foreign dude, a Samaritan. At this time, the Jews in Israel and neighboring Samaritans hated each other, fighting wars, murdering each other's caravans, and vandalizing neighboring churches. This was serious anger. I imagine it's pretty similar to the current Israel-Palestine situation.

Jesus, documented in the Book of Luke, tells a story about this Jewish guy on the road. He'd been robbed and beaten within an inch of his life, and left to die. Two other Jews just walked on by but this enemy Samaritan, though, turned out to be a good guy. He stopped, got the guy cleaned up, and paid for a hotel room so he could rest and heal.

The moral of the story? The dude who doesn't look or

act like us, the "Good Samaritan," becomes our neighbor by treating us with kindness and compassion.

It doesn't stop there, though. During the time of Jesus, the Romans had invaded and made Israel part of their empire. Initially, things were cool, but eventually they got so bad that Jews rose up and fought several wars against them. Jesus, though, taught compassion for everyone and lived that life himself. When a Roman soldier came and asked him to heal a buddy, Jesus talked to the guy, went to his house, and healed his friend. He said of the soldier, "I tell you, I have not found such great faith even in Israel."

Jesus asked that we treat everyone with compassion, kindness, forgiveness, and acceptance, making crystal clear that this lesson always includes "foreigners." This glee that we see from right-wing Christian Nationalist folks who only want to be surrounded by folks like them?

Jesus is strongly on the other side of that argument.

The Bible and Consistency

So many bros will quote Bible verses when they want to back up their views. Two of the most common are from the non-Gospel parts of the Bible, so not directly involved with Jesus' life, and are used to defend laws restricting people's rights. The problem for these dudes is that the Bible can be pretty inconsistent.

In the Old Testament book of Leviticus it states that, "You shall not lie with a male as with a woman. It is an abomination." Tom Ascol, a Florida pastor who prayed over Governor Ron Desantis when he was sworn in as the state's governor, loudly proclaims that this Bible verse makes it OK to give gay people the death penalty.

Another one we've talked a lot about in this book is from the New Testament book of Ephesians, which gives instructions to women in marriage: "Wives, submit to your own husbands, as to the Lord." This is used for all sorts of proposals by right-wing guys hoping to hamstring women who just want to be equals in our communities. The biggest recent example is that push we've talked about to remove women's right to vote.

The funny thing is I never hear these guys being as passionate about other parts of the Bible. So if you ever hear someone spouting this stuff, ask them how they feel about the following:

Tattoos: In the same book of Leviticus used to defend the murder of gay people, direction is pretty clear about tattoos. "Do not cut your bodies for the dead or put tattoo marks on yourselves. I am the LORD."

Shellfish: Leviticus also makes it pretty clear which fish you are and are NOT supposed to eat. "...anything that doesn't have fins or scales—whether from the seas or the rivers—any of the swarming creatures and living creatures in the waters are detestable for you. They are to remain detestable for you. You are not to eat of their meat." I hate to tell you, but that means shrimp, lobster, mussels, and scallops are all a no-no according to the Bible.

Widows and Brothers: Dudes with brothers, if your bro gets married but dies before his wife has a son, guess what? According to the Bible, you're supposed to marry her now! And if you don't, the widow can confront you in public, spit in your face, hit you with a shoe, and if you have any kids with a new woman, you will now be known as the "Family of the Unsandled."

Yeah, seriously.

There is plenty more stuff in the Old Testament, but let's talk about New Testament stories after the Gospels.

Fellas, you want long hair? Sorry, dude. If you grow your hair out it is a "disgrace to you."

How about getting your girlfriend or wife a nice gold ring or a pearl necklace? Nope. Women need to "dress modestly" without expensive clothes or jewelry.

Ephesians, the same book that gives us rules about wives submitting, also has something to say about, well, slavery. Specifically, it's a good thing. "Slaves, obey your earthly masters with respect and fear, and with sincerity of heart, just as you would obey Christ."

Conclusion

The Bible is a book. It's a really well-meaning one with some amazing life lessons, focusing on a really good guy trying to convince us all to be better people. Ask yourself, though, about the people using it as a justification for their morals.

Are they about violence, hatred, getting rich, or putting others down to feel better? Are they from dudes flaunting cross tattoos, buying gaudy jewelry for their wives, and enjoying lobster on the weekend, but threatening the rights of women and gay folks and taking away health care and food from the poor?

If so, is this consistent with the guy the religion is, you know, named after?

For me, love, kindness, giving, forgiveness, and loving my neighbor as myself are the biggies that I take away from Jesus' word.

That's the good shit, man. Let's do this stuff more.

CHAPTER 27

Trump and the Death of Responsibility

So many things about Donald Trump piss me off. There are the sexual assaults, all of the Epstein shit, his making fun of disabled people, screwing over his workers, insulting veterans, and using the Presidency as some weird infomercial to sell shit with his name on it (Bibles, shoes, meme coins, cologne, etc.). All of this makes me question how people can view him as a real man.

Making matters worse, as the top public official in the country, he is now a role model to countless young men who view this garbage as not only acceptable but something to strive for. His portrayal of a "masculine movement" appeals to many dudes who have missed out on real, responsible mentors.

Honestly though? The one thing that gets my blood boiling most is his inability to take responsibility.

My dad, Lt. Col. McCamley, U.S. Army (Ret.), was not good at expressing emotion. We talked about this in a past chapter, and how figuring that out late in life was one of the toughest, bravest things he ever did for our family.

You know what my dad was always amazing at though? Taking responsibility.

He paid the bills, saved for the future, changed the oil in the car regularly, gave to charity, and never got a speeding ticket. Not one.

He also made *damn sure* his kids knew the importance of all of this stuff. My sister and I had the word "responsibility" tattooed on our souls before we left the house. I truly believe that this is one of the biggest reasons she and I both got jobs trying to help people, me in politics and her in health care. Taking responsibility to make our communities better always meant more to us than just getting a ton of money.

But when Trump, and the people around him, refuse to do the same thing, it sends a terrible message to the young men in this country about the importance of one of the most masculine of values.

The two most obvious areas where this is a problem? Trump's inability to ever admit he is wrong, and his lack of accountability as a leader.

Apologizing

I am a goalkeeper. I've played the position at various levels for hockey, soccer, and even Gaelic football teams. The last is an Irish game…think a combination of soccer, basketball, and rugby. It is mentally tough because when there is a goal, it always feels like it's on you. Also, you throw your body in the way of a ball or puck shot as hard as possible, which gives us all a reputation for being nuts.

There is another big job with goalkeeping though, and that is communication. From goal, we see the whole field or rink. While another teammate has to focus on one specific player, we have to be aware of the whole field of play so we can direct defenders to where open opposition players are moving to. That requires a lot of trust.

Sometimes, I screw up. I may not communicate well with my defenders, might not be aggressive enough coming up to smother the ball or puck, or just have a stupid brain freeze and let something through my legs. Feel free to bring on the jokes about the last thing. I've heard them all.

I hate it when these things happen, but when it is my fault, *it is super important for me to apologize*. I need my teammates to know that I understand where I fucked up, and that they can trust me to do better. If they lose that trust and overcompensate by trying to do things I normally would, the team gets all out of shape. Then you lose.

Even more importantly, I need to know internally that what I did wasn't good enough and that *I need to get better*. That is the type of accountability that fuels personal improvement, a masculine quality for all sorts of life situations.

Apologizing is the ultimate form of taking the responsibility to improve. It's hard, but I know my old man would be proud of me whenever I do it.

You see this happen in pro sports all of the time. LeBron James, Patrick Mahomes, Tom Brady? Every single one of them takes responsibility for mistakes after wins AND losses.

Trump doesn't believe in any of this. One of his earliest influences was a lawyer named Roy Cohn. Cohn started his professional life as a staffer to Sen Joseph McCarthy, a guy described as "the single most despised man in American political memory" because of his calling Americans of all varieties communists during the 1950's Red Scare. Cohn later represented the five biggest New York crime families, the Catholic church, and a young real estate developer looking to evade a lawsuit from black people because he refused to rent to them: Donald Trump.

He drilled Trump on his strategy of dealing with life. Attack first when you can. When you can't, make your counterattack 100 times worse. And never, ever say you're sorry.

To Trump, apologizing is the "biggest show of weakness" possible and only gives enemies a way to attack you. He has said the most vile, hateful, offensive things possible and the only instance of him ever even coming close to saying the word "sorry" is after the *Access Hollywood* tapes came out during the 2016 election. He bragged about being able to grab women by the pussy, which without their consent is sexual assault. Even then, he refused to take responsibility for his actions, saying: "This was locker room banter, a private conversation that took place many years ago. Bill Clinton has said far worse to me on the golf course—not even close. I apologize if anyone was offended."

There is actually a term for "I apologize if anyone was offended." It's called a non-apology apology, where someone refuses to take responsibility for their actions and shifts the blame for any feelings to the person who "was offended."

Trump once said on Jimmy Fallon's show, "I will absolutely apologize sometime in the hopefully distant future if

I'm ever wrong." Since he's never done it, he must think he's perfect.

But no one is perfect, which makes what Trump says weak and small. Neither you nor your team can get better unless you admit you were wrong when you screw up. And refusing to improve because it is hard is something Col. McCamley would hold in the absolute lowest of regards.

Leadership

There is an old saying for when no one wants to take responsibility for something: "Pass The Buck." It comes from poker games in the 1800s. The responsibility for dealing rotates around the table. Back then, to show whose turn it was, there was a buck-handled knife placed in front of them. On your turn, if you didn't want to deal, you would put the knife in front of the next person or Pass the Buck.

President Harry Truman made some of the toughest decisions in American history. He gave the order to drop the atomic bombs on Japan and end WWII, took the lead in creating the North Atlantic Treaty Organization (NATO) with Europe, and desegregated the military.

In the Oval Office, Truman had a sign on his desk that said, "The Buck Stops Here." He described why that was important to him, saying, "The President—whoever he is—has to decide. He can't pass the buck to anybody. No one else can do the deciding for him. That's his job."

Leaders have to make decisions, and good ones take responsibility for all of them, whether they work or not.

In early 1960, President Dwight Eisenhower planned an invasion of Cuba using CIA-trained Cuban exiles who fled to Florida after Castro took over. John F. Kennedy took over as President in 1961 and three months later, the "Bay of Pigs" invasion happened. It was a massive failure. Though JFK could have blamed Eisenhower or the CIA publicly, he didn't.

Instead, he publicly took responsibility, saying, "Victory has 100 fathers and defeat is an orphan....I am the responsible officer of the government." He then fired a bunch of people and reorganized the CIA.

In 1987, President Ronald Reagan was deeply involved in the Iran Contra scandal. It was a complicated scheme where some of Reagan's high-ranking government officials sold missiles to Iran, where the Ayatollah had just taken over in a bloody revolution and called the U.S. the "Great Satan." The government officials thought selling the missiles to Iran would convince them to release some U.S. hostages being held in Lebanon. The proceeds from the sale were then used to fund an anti-Communist group of revolutionaries in Nicaragua, the Contras.

Reagan said publicly that there was "no arms for hostages"...until it came out in the news that was exactly what was going on. Reagan replied, "A few months ago, I told the American people I did not trade arms for hostages. My heart and my best intentions still tell me that's true, but the facts and the evidence tell me it is not...I take full responsibility for my own actions and for those of my administration." He then fired a bunch of people and commissioned an independent report that criticized Reagan for not properly supervising his employees.

You don't need to be president to show responsibility in leadership. In the spring of 2020, as COVID was starting to take hold of the world, there was an outbreak on the aircraft carrier *USS Theodore Roosevelt*. The ship was routed to a base in Guam, in the Indian Ocean, where only 100 or so crew were taken off. The Captain of the ship, Brett Crozier, asked that all of his crew be removed to help control the spread and save lives. He was denied, but that didn't stop him. He sent a four-page memo to ten admirals, going above his two immediate superiors, pleading for the safety of his crew. The letter was leaked to the *San Francisco Chronicle*, who printed it and generated the pressure necessary to evacuate the ship.

Crozier was relieved of his command, but after all the crew was tested, it was found 660 of the sailors (including Crozier himself) were positive for COVID. Getting them off the ship saved lives. The buck stopped with him, and he took responsibility with a decision that ended his career.

An interesting thing about all of this? People like it when leaders take responsibility for bad things as well as good stuff. JFK saw his popularity go up after his press conference on the Bay of Pigs. Reagan saw the Iran Contra affair tank his approval numbers, but after his statement saw his popularity rebound into positive territory. And Crozier? The sailors under his command cheered him as he left the *Roosevelt* after being fired.

Trump as President, on the other hand, never seems to have met a tough situation he didn't want to run away from as fast as possible.

- While Captain Crozier took responsibility for his crew, making a tough decision to try and save lives, Trump responded to delays in COVID tests, saying, "I don't take any responsibility at all." He kept blaming Obama and the nature of the virus itself, saying, "No one could have foreseen this."

- In 2017, after a failed operation in Yemen that led to the death of a Navy SEAL, Trump was no JFK. Instead of taking responsibility, he blamed the generals and the previous administration, saying, "My generals... lost Ryan" and that the decision was made "before I got here."

- Over and over, when the stock market has done well, Trump hasn't hesitated to take credit. In January of 2024, when prices were up, he called it the "Trump Stock Market" because he claimed to be winning in the polls. In April of 2024, when prices were slumping, it became "Bidenomics." He did the same thing in 2017, taking credit when prices were up, and blaming the Federal Reserve in 2018 when they crashed.

- After the January 6th attempted coup on the Capitol, which occurred immediately after Trump riled up an already angry crowd and told them to go to the Capitol, Trump shifted any responsibility to his Vice President, Mike Pence. "You can blame him," Trump said after rioters erected a guillotine for Pence with the message clear that they literally wanted to cut his head off. He was no Reagan.

- Before his Presidency, Trump's casinos in Atlantic City went bankrupt repeatedly, underperforming compared to others around him and leaving him billions of dollars in debt. He never took responsibility for these, giving himself raises while blaming former executives who died in a helicopter crash.

When the Trump tariffs were put in place, he blamed other countries for the problems created for American farmers. When top secret documents were illegally found at his Mar A Lago mansion, he claimed that the FBI planted them.

Nothing is ever on him, unless it's good. He always passes the buck. And according to President Truman, that shit makes you less of a real man.

As men, our decisions matter. We only have credibility with those around us if we take responsibility for our actions when they work *and* when they don't.

Real dudes aren't afraid to man up when we screw up. We should know the importance of responsibility to the teams around us, and understand that improving means acknowledging where we need work to get better.

CHAPTER 28

Conquest vs Competition

John Eldridge's book, *Wild at Heart Revised and Updated: Discovering the Secret of a Man's Soul*, has been required reading for many Christian men's groups over the last two decades. In it, he advocates for a more "manly" view of Christianity, telling men to act like a "warrior" and that "Deep in his heart, every man longs for a battle to fight, an adventure to live, and a beauty to rescue."

According to Eldridge, modern life has been set up to take us down. He quotes the 1800s book *Iron John*, saying, "Some women want a passive man if they want a man at all; the church wants a tamed man—they are called priests; the university wants a domesticated man—they are called tenure-track people; the corporation wants a...sanitized, hairless, shallow man."

Women are only things: a "beauty to rescue," "fair maiden," or "damsel in distress." In another book of his, *Captivating: Unveiling the Mystery of a Woman's Soul*, he says that every woman has three core values: to be romanced, to play an implacable role in a great adventure, and to unveil beauty. Their sole role is a target to be swept away and cared for, but not recognized as a whole person.

To be fair, many men DO want a mission making us feel like part of something bigger. I know I do. But dig a little deeper into Eldridge and other guys like this, and a man's main goal becomes more about another word: conquest.

Conquest and Domination

Accused rapist Andrew Tate has a message for men who are experiencing depression. "There's a rebel inside of every man and men have an innate desire for adventure and conquest to a degree. You're not going to feel good as a man unless you're conquering something."

He goes farther than that, refusing to "forgive my enemies until they've suffered." He claims women "literally beg" for the "famous human trafficker bad guy" with money. And he talks over and over about wealth not being a tool for happiness, but a means of power over others.

Tate, however, is far from the only manosphere contributor who lives for conquest.

Remember Doug Wilson, the pastor who took a flamethrower to Elsa from *Frozen*? In his Book Fidelity: *What it Means to be a One-Woman Man* he says "the sexual act cannot be made into an egalitarian pleasuring party. A man penetrates, conquers, colonizes, plants. A woman receives, surrenders, accepts."

Right wing political commentator Matt Walsh calls for the "glorious conquest of Canada" by the United States and says Native Americans shouldn't have any right to

Reservation land anymore because they "got conquered. OK? It happens."

Conservative pastor George Grant is the author of *The Changing of the Guard: Biblical Blueprints for Political Action*. In it, he says the mission of "Christian politics has as its primary intent the conquest of the land, of men, families, institutions, bureaucracies, courts, and governments for the kingdom of Christ."

Ben Shapiro has made a living going to college campuses, "debating" people less experienced than himself. He then puts short clips making him look good online with titles like "Ben Shapiro DESTROYS Ignorant College Student."

To these guys, a real man only truly defines himself by dominating something else. A woman, another man's bank account, other countries you don't agree with, a person with darker skin coming from a different part of the world, or a much less experienced college student.

But here's the thing, none of this leads you to a place of internal peace.

JD Rockefeller was one of the world's wealthiest people and first oil oligarch. Today, he would be like an Elon Musk or Jeff Bezos. A reporter found time to talk to him in the early 1900s, and asked how much money it takes to make a man happy. Rockefeller's famous reply? "Just a little more."

Apparently, even a guy like Rockefeller, whose whole life was about acquiring wealth (Rockefeller Center, in New York City, was built by his son) found some wisdom enough to admit something profound. All of his money and stuff never made him truly content.

As for dominating other countries, that doesn't really work either.

- Soviet dictator Joseph Stalin was one of the world's most powerful men for decades. However, in his last years he was described as a "lonely old man" who distrusted doctors, feared everyone was going to poison him, hardly slept, and almost never left his rural house because of fear.
- Adolf Hitler was a famous druggie, using meth, oxy, and cocaine regularly. He died by shooting himself in the head, while his longtime girlfriend took a cyanide pill next to him.
- China's dictator, Mao Zedong, lived through long periods of depression. His own doctor described him as becoming withdrawn, spending long times in bed, and avoiding sunlight.

Rape

Research and interviews with convicted rapists and their victims show that when men rape women, it's not just about sex. "I wanted to show her who was boss" and "It wasn't about sex—it was about getting respect." These are common statements suggesting a need for men to get revenge against women or punish them for perceived past injustices. It's important to note that rape victims, including men, are overwhelmingly young. So rapists exert power and control over people they find attractive, in the form of sex, to satiate a drive that they aren't getting consensually.

In a United Nations report documenting rape during war, one of the generals interviewed said, "It is perhaps more dangerous to be a woman than a soldier in an armed conflict." The Red Cross studies the use of rape during war, and found that armies use it as a strategy to dominate and subjugate populations, in addition to being a sexual reward for the male soldiers.

Eldridge's take on life, Wilson's ideas about sex being conquest, and all the "Women submit to your husband" guys don't help dissuade these violent ideas. The more you take away another's humanity as full people, making them into an object or thing, the easier it is to do horrendous shit to them.

Maybe Andrew Tate's need to "conquer" to prove his worth as a man is a reason he is being investigated for rape in Romania and England, and why the Attorney General in Florida is looking into Tate because he "publicly admitted to participating in what very much appears to be soliciting, trafficking, preying upon women around the world."

Competition and Conflict

There is a big difference, though, between conquest and competition.

Competition and conflict can be great things. The pressure that comes from any kind of opponent, be it in sports, a job interview, or a fundraiser forces us to work and think in a manner that we wouldn't normally do.

The hardest I've ever worked were in life experiences spurred by contests.

I'm 4-3 in runs for elected office. For every single race, knowing I only had a certain amount of time to learn as much as possible about current topics people cared about, talk to as many voters as I could, and create a message that broke through made me work my ass off. Even if you do these things, you can still lose. But lazy candidates don't come out on the winning end most times.

COVID was a different kind of opponent. I knew that eventually pandemics wear off as viruses evolve. The challenge there was to fight for a system that made it bearable for people to stay home as much as possible. The opponent here was no person, but the country's third largest murderer in 2020 and 2021.

I am not the only one that views competitions as something humans need to thrive.

Regarding hard work, comedian and TV host Drew Carey says, "Some people don't like competition because it makes them work harder, better." Retired General and Secretary of State Colin Powell comments that "The healthiest competition occurs when average people win by putting [in] above average effort." Whole Foods founder John Mackey reports that "competition forces companies to get out of their complacency."

NBA champion Kevin Garnett mentions how competition spurs understanding, saying, "I've always been driven by the competition and the learning process." Rock and Roll Hall of Fame member Patti Smith takes that one step further. "An artist is somebody who enters into competition with God," she says, giving her a better understanding of the human spirit.

Probably my favorite quote about competition, though, comes from sports commentator Howard Cosell, who covered *Monday Night Football*, multiple Olympics, the rise of Mohammad Ali, and the death of John Lennon. He said in his book *I Never Played the Game*, "The ultimate victory in competition is derived from the inner satisfaction of knowing that you have done your best and that you have gotten the most out of what you had to give."

Cosell does a great job here of breaking down the difference between the healthy pressure of competition, and assholes like Tate who distort it. Real, healthy men understand that the pressure of competing makes us better on the inside. Strong men don't need to put their boot on someone's neck to define their success. They don't need to "own" anyone to prove their masculinity.

That is for weak men like Tate.

Real men understand that risk-taking, putting yourself out there, competing against a quality opponent, and learning from those experiences so you can get better is what makes us strong.

Conquering the Right Things

So my dudes, we're probably all guys that like a mission. We enjoy being given a quest. Most of us like a little healthy competition. So if we feel the need to conquer, let's focus on dominating problems rather than people.

We've talked extensively about the problems men are facing with our mental and spiritual health. Why don't we start with conquering our internal demons? Conquering them means doing hard things...putting down our phones, hanging out with friends in real life, being comfortable with expressing our emotions when they come out, and asking for help when we need it. That means taking some risks, but the rewards will almost always outweigh the uncomfortable stuff that can come from being proactive.

How about our economic situations? We can help conquer our fiscal futures by not only working hard, but also by getting our education levels up and choosing jobs that we know will be around and not taken up by AI or robots. Getting out of your comfort zone and into class and jobs where we may be a minority might be a tough thing to start, but it will likely give you massive returns.

We can also conquer our addiction to spending money on shit that doesn't leave us feeling better, but does make us broke. Going overboard on sports betting, drugs, AI girlfriends, or OnlyFans might give you a short period of good feelings. But, they leave you worse off long-term and that shit sure does dominate your bank account.

We can conquer the loneliness, frustration, and anger in the boys around us by being role models. Getting a job in a school, becoming a sports coach or Big Brother, or even just checking in regularly on the young guys in your neighborhood are all ways to show boys that they are cared for and belong in the world. This gets you on the team that can defeat the growing epidemic of suicide and mass shootings that are becoming so common...and will also probably make you feel better.

In the bigger political picture, why do we need to invade other countries? We can Make America Great Again by dominating problems that lead to better lives. We used to fight poverty, Nazis, and disease. The U.S. conquered the sky and then space, slayed slavery, beat the shit out of illiteracy and ignorance, and helped to crush smallpox. Our universities became the envy of the free world. American bridges and dams saved countless lives, and we invented the fucking internet...which helped to bring the world together.

Let's get back to doing shit like that.

Some guys think they can be like Tate by going online and trolling other people with one-line insults. But calling someone a homo because you don't agree with them doesn't do anything for you, or the world around you. Honestly, I see guys like this and I feel sorry for them.

But engaging in real competition, where you work hard, learn, grow and improve yourself also makes the world around us better.

So fellas, let's get in the fight for the right things and become better men at the same time.

CHAPTER 29

Interviews with Interesting Guys
DAVID MORALES

David really cares about kids. And so many have benefited from his work.

He didn't go to college right away. As an assistant high school coach, he applied for the full-time job when it opened up, but was turned down because he wasn't a teacher. After five years of sobriety recovering from alcohol and drug addiction, that was the spark that led him back to school and then a lifetime teaching.

Now at twenty-one years of serving kids, David's commitment to young people has been recognized at the highest levels. He was recognized as the state Teacher of the Year in 2016, and received a Golden Apple in Excellence teaching award in 2024. The son of immigrants, David runs his school's ENLACE program. Originally started to prepare first generation Hispanic students for college, he has expanded his college prep work for kids of all races and backgrounds. He's coached boys and girls soccer for decades, and still plays in recreational leagues.

Coming from a wealth of experience and knowledge, he shares some critical life lessons.

Becoming a Teacher

"I've been sober for nearly thirty-two years now, and when I decided to become a teacher, I had been sober for about five or six years. Everything was still fresh in my mind. All the mistakes I had made and all the things I had done wrong were right there in front of me. I remember thinking, 'You know what? If I can help just one kid avoid making the same mistakes I made, if I can help one kid not throw their hands up and say, "Forget it," then maybe it's worth it.' So I went back to school.

"I drank and drugged myself out of college when I was nineteen. I eventually went back when I was about twenty-nine or thirty. My wife had also gone back to school, so we were both full-time students raising three kids. I was coaching two soccer teams and working full-time, and she was working full-time as well. We were on Medicaid and food stamps, using every available resource as a tool to help us get where we wanted to be. At the same time, it was one of the most challenging periods of my life and one of the most rewarding."

Boys and Education

"When I talk to boys, one of the questions I always ask is, 'What's going to happen after I call your name at graduation?' When they step off that stage, I want them to think about what comes next.

"I have students tell me, 'I want to be a mechanic.' Great. My dad was an auto mechanic, and my brother is too. They've done very well for themselves. There's honor and pride in that work. But then I ask them, 'Wouldn't you rather be engineering those cars?' It's about planting seeds and helping them understand that they are capable of more than they may believe.

"A lot of boys think, 'This is all I can do,' or, 'I'm expected to make money and help support my family.' They feel pressure to become providers right away. So we talk about what kind of lifestyle they want and what kind of education or training it takes to build that life if they truly want to provide for the people they care about."

The Mentor's Role

"I can't be their friend. We can be friendly, but not friends. At least, not until after you cross that stage. Sometimes I have to be the one to tell them the hard truth because I don't want them to make the same mistakes I made. I'll ask them, 'Do you want me to tell you what you want to hear, or do you want me to tell you the truth? Do you want me to fix this, or do you just need me to listen?' And they'll tell you.

"When students come to me asking for advice, I challenge them. I want to tell them, 'Pull your head out. But what I ask is, What are you thinking about? How is the decision you're making right now going to affect your future?' Every decision has an impact later on. I also remind them not to let a temporary emotion make a permanent decision.

"I explain it to them this way: 'Right now, you're still early in your story. You might be in chapter fourteen. I'm somewhere around chapter fifty. I've lived long enough to have a pretty good idea how certain decisions turn out, and I'm trying to help guide you toward better ones.' I tell them, 'Go to school. Try it. And if you decide it's not for you, fine. But at least you'll never have to look back and wonder 'What if?''

"I have one student who's getting ready to leave for the Marines. Great kid. Tough when he needs to be and softhearted when he needs to be. I love that balance in him. But I told him, 'You still need to fill out college applications and scholarships.' He said, 'Mister, I'm not going to college. I'm joining the military.' I told him, 'Okay, but you walk to school, right? What if a bus hits you between now and then? What have you prepared for?'

"That's what love looks like to me. Love isn't always congratulating someone and telling them what they want to hear. Sometimes love is pushing people to do things they don't want to do because you know it's what's best for them. That's how you model positive love without making it unrealistic or superficial.

"Boys often come to me to ask about relationships. I ask them, 'Are you becoming the best version of yourself for the person you hope to be with someday? Are you building yourself into someone worthy of that relationship?'"

Sharing Emotions

"In our class, we create opportunities for students to socialize and connect with each other. One of the activities we do is called Circle. Honestly, it makes me nervous sometimes because I never know what students are going to say or what I'll have to respond to. But the students love it.

"They love it because it gives them a safe environment where they can choose how much they want to share. Nothing is forced. They can pass if they want to, but when the questions are meaningful, they usually open up.

"For a lot of our boys, especially, Circle gives them permission to cry, to share, and to talk about the things that hurt them. That doesn't happen immediately. It takes time for students to feel safe enough to be vulnerable. But once they do, they begin letting things out instead of carrying everything inside. And when those moments happen, the phones suddenly become secondary because students want to be fully present with each other."

Having A Strong Partner

"One of the qualities I wanted most in a partner was intelligence. I wanted somebody who could challenge me intellectually, ask the right questions, push me, and still make me laugh. My wife does all of those things constantly.

"I never wanted somebody to be submissive to me. I wanted a true partner, somebody who would challenge me because I grew up surrounded by strong women. My mom was a homemaker, but she was incredibly strong. My sister is strong too and earned her own degree. That shaped the way I viewed relationships.

"My wife and I still challenge each other all the time, and I wouldn't want it any other way. If I had advice for someone who wants a traditional relationship where their wife simply submits to them, I'd say they'll probably get bored pretty quickly. And so will she."

The Need for Mentors

Jay Shorter worked for thirty years in Northern VA's Prince William County as a PE teacher and coach. While he spent most of his time on basketball and football, he started a tennis team at Woodbridge Middle School which I was fortunate enough to play on in the 8th grade.

My middle school years, like so many kids,' were tough. I didn't fit in well, got made fun of a lot, and felt super awkward most of the time. But Jay was one of the few male teachers I had, and he did a tremendous job with the mostly white, middle-class boys he had under his wing. When I was thirteen, he was one of the best male role models outside of my old man that I had, and his effort is appreciated to this day.

After retiring, he moved back to his roots in southwest DC, becoming a volunteer basketball coach at Jefferson Middle School Academy. He also runs a non-profit called DC Storm that supplements the school's team. He starts boys on his program in the summer, where the coaches can develop relationships with the kids and the team can travel for games before the regular school league starts later in the fall. These students are not in the same demographic that I grew up with in Virginia. They are majority black, their families don't make as much money, and most come from single-parent households.

I was fortunate to visit Jay recently at a high school fair where his kids got to see all of their choices for the next stage in their education. We were in the school gym, filled with laughing, excited students. His boys though? They all proactively came up to "Coach Jay" to shake his hand. Everyone was respectful, engaged, and successful. I know the last thing is true because I asked all of them how their grades were, and almost every one of them responded with "Honor Roll." It was honestly really impressive.

See, Jay meets with these kids from 3:00-5:00 p.m. after school, every day, to do homework. Basketball practice starts after, but the kids know if they don't keep their grades up, they don't play. They also have to be respectful on social media. You talk shit about opponents online, you don't keep your place on the team.

He also uses these sessions to check on their home situations, making sure they are doing well outside of school. He told me about a situation where the mother of one of his kids called him once asking for help. They had just moved to town and she was in an abusive relationship. Jay helped her find a place she could move to and not get the shit kicked out of her every day. This was better for the mom AND the kid.

There is a saying he uses over and over: *"If kids don't think that you care, they won't care what you think."* He is passionate about the need for mentors to actively engage with these boys and show them that they have meaning and value. Jay believes strongly that investing in relationships with these kids is the thing that makes the real difference in their lives...like he did with me.

Another gentleman I got to meet was Andrew Barnes, the head basketball coach from nearby Ballou High School who was there recruiting. When we spoke, he mentioned that there were three qualities any mentor needed to be effective with boys: Accountability. Authenticity. Consistency.

Role models need to hold kids accountable for both the good and bad things they may do. If you don't give them praise AND make sure they know when they screw up, they won't respect you. Secondly, kids today value authenticity more than anything. They need to know you are real or they won't listen to you. Third, and maybe most importantly, you need to be consistent in being there for them. Just showing up once doesn't cut it in the long-term lives of these kids, and abandoning them, as we'll see a little later, can leave them feeling and doing worse.

The Role Model Problem

Why are these stories important? Because one of the biggest problems boys and young men have in today's communities is a lack of good role models. Barack Obama has been one of the fiercest voices for more male mentors. Early in his presidency, he hosted a Town Hall on fatherhood, saying, "We need dads—but also men who aren't dads—to serve as mentors. Even if it's just for a couple hours a week of shooting hoops, or helping with homework, or just talking. Even the smallest moments can have an enormous impact on a child's life." In launching an initiative called My Brother's Keeper, he specifically asked men to take up these roles: "We are going to need more of you to be mentors and role models and supporters for this next generation...then we're going to call on them to reach back and invest in the folks who are coming behind them."

Obama isn't the only one asking for more male mentors. LeBron James has called on more athletes to mentor young men. Former football player, action star, and sexual assault survivor Terry Crews testified before Congress about how we need good guy mentors to break the cycle of sexual assault and current mental health crisis. Denzel Washington has given multiple presentations on the need for more fellas to mentor young men, and Avengers' Chris Evans (Captain America) and Mark Ruffalo (The Incredible Hulk) have asked Hollywood to normalize characters that get therapy and display more empathy, respectively.

The reason all of these dudes are speaking out on the issue? It really, really matters.

Fatherhood

When a father leaves a family, boys are much less likely to grow with the full range of emotions and values they need for good mental health. The problems get worse the earlier in life the boy doesn't have his old man around. Other effects of dad taking off are increases in "risky behavior" like acting out, early smoking, or getting girls pregnant leading to more school dropouts. Some research also points out that when a dude grows up without a dad, he is more likely to experience mental health issues when he becomes an adult.

Why is this such a massive issue in the United States? 23% of kids grow up in a home with only one parent (almost always the mom). This is the highest rate in the world.

Teachers

We've talked extensively about the lack of male teachers in our schools. In 1988, 30% of teachers were fellas. That number is down to 23% and continues to drop. Only 26% of Language Arts high school teachers are men (as compared to over 50% of PE teachers). Boys across racial and economic groups consistently read and write at a poorer level than girls. This is a problem.

I am 48, and can still name all of my male school teachers. Mr. Penn was my 5th grade science teacher for one semester before he got promoted to assistant principal. Mr. Anderson in Algebra and Mr. Shorter (see above) for PE both taught me in 8th grade. In high school, I had Mr. Andrews for Algebra 2, Mr. Scroggs for World History, Mr. Shock for Biology, Mr.

Castetter for Chemistry, Mr. Smith for U.S. History, and Mr Schutz for Band. Hell, I even still remember Mr. Wong, one of the regular substitutes at Mayfield High.

Teacher representation matters, and if a guy like me still remembers all of his male teachers, you know it leaves an impact.

Outside Mentors

Mentoring outside of the classroom also is needed. Research shows that when a kid has a Big Brother or Big Sister, they are much less likely to be depressed or have conduct problems and more likely to do better at school. Maybe even more importantly, they *believe that they are smarter*. Kids that had a Big Brother or Sister were more likely to attend college, and earn 15% more than a comparable set of kids that didn't have a mentor.

Other studies show that when kids are mentored, they are less likely to use drugs, start drinking, or get into fights. They are more likely to do better in school than kids who don't have mentors.

So What Can You Do?

Fellas, as Obama and LeBron said, we need you. In addition to a shortage of male teachers, there are also waiting lists for boys in Big Brothers programs. The study above actually mentioned that some of the boys had to have women mentors because of a lack of male volunteers. The organization reports a constant shortage of male mentors, with 70% of kids on their waitlist being boys, and many waiting months or years for a match.

If you have any interest in being a Big Brother, it is very easy to get started. Just go to their website, and enter your zip code to find out where the closest office is.

Just make sure that if you take this step, you can consistently meet with the kid you are matched with. As Coach Barnes said in the first part of this chapter, consistency is key to any mentor relationship. If kids only get you for six months, they probably won't see any improvement. And when mentors cut out after only three months, kids actually do worse than if you weren't there at all.

Other groups out there offering structural mentoring programs include:

- **Boys and Girls Clubs of America.** After-school clubs nationwide offering sports, arts, and leadership programs where kids aged 6-18 interact with male staff/volunteers as role models.
- **Boys to Men Mentoring Network**. A nationwide network offering group-based mentoring for boys aged 12-18. They focus on building integrity, accountability, and emotional intelligence through weekly school meetings, retreats, and peer support.
- **Becoming a Man (BAM) Program**. Available in eight major cities, this program needs co-facilitators for groups of boys from the 7th-12th grades.

And there are plenty of regional organizations as well. The Journeyman group in North Carolina and Champs mentoring project in Chicago are two examples of ways to get involved in smaller but effective groups helping boys.

If you have a Bachelor's degree, you can also teach in school. This can be as little as a few times a month as a substitute, or you can go all in and get a full-time job. Districts across the country are desperate for teachers, as last year there were over 45,000 positions vacant with another 366,000 filled with full time substitutes or people unqualified for the positions. If you are interested, Teach.org has some great resources and their recent webinar "Men Who Teach" offers some great insights into the profession.

I recently signed up to substitute teach in my hometown. There was an all-day training, followed by some video education on everything from fire extinguishers to bullying. Then, they get you in the classroom. My first two classes were 8th grade orchestra. Yes, I "conducted" using my high school and college drummer experience. The boys did seem to appreciate having a fella in front, and I got asked by one guy how much protein powder I took on a daily basis.

It's important to close this chapter with two things.

First, mentoring doesn't just have to happen in a structured environment. Taking the time to check in on your neighbors' sons on a regular basis can let them know there are people out there looking out for them.

Second, this isn't about just helping boys, either. If you have an opportunity to reach out to a young man at work, it could be an opportunity to lend a helping hand and provide support for how to navigate the place using your experience. Or, another dude in your neighborhood might enjoy watching a game and getting a drink on the weekend. This could be a great opportunity to provide some real connection that will make both of you feel better.

At the end of the day, this isn't hard. It just takes some proactivity and time. But if we all reach out and do our part, we can help other fellas do better. And this will make us healthier, happier, and more fulfilled as well.

CHAPTER 31

Expertise

The Beatles had a hell of an eight-year run. The music they made between signing their first major recording contract in 1962 and their breakup in 1970 made them the best-selling band of all time. *The Guinness Book of*  *Records* sets their number of units sold (records, tapes, CD's, etc.) as 1 billion. Yes, billion with a B.

To put this in perspective, compare these numbers to the most popular artists of today. Taylor Swift? The highest estimate of her sales is 137 million, and she's been going for twenty years. The biggest number available for Drake is 500 million, and he's been putting out music for almost twenty-five years.

The Beatles didn't just show up out of thin air being good, though. Before they made it big, they left their hometown of Liverpool in England and played little clubs in Germany for two years. Their first gigs were in a place called the Indra

Club, for a handful of people who were mostly sex workers and their clients. They stayed in rooms behind a cheap theater without showers or heat, and got paid $2.50 per dude, per day. They didn't get famous or make a ton of money in Hamburg, but they got something else that proved to be super valuable.

Practice

John Lennon described it by saying, "We had to play for hours and hours on end. Every song lasted twenty minutes and had twenty solos in it. That's what improved the playing. There was nobody to copy from. We played what we liked best and the Germans liked it as long as it was loud." They had to compete with other bands for stage time, and changed their look a couple of times...going from leather jackets and ducktails to the famous suit, tie, and mod haircut look that made them famous in 1964.

To use a sports term, they got their reps in.

Steph Curry is the best pure shooter in NBA history, and one of the greatest basketball players ever. He's been an All Star 11 times, has four NBA Championship rings (in two of those he was Finals MVP), and has been the League's most valuable player in two seasons as well. In the 2024 Olympic Gold Medal game against France on their home floor, he led the USA to victory with twenty-four points. Twelve of these were in the closing moments, one of which was an absolute dagger over two defenders to ice the win...after which he celebrated with his trademark "nite nite" motion to a rabid crowd.

Curry's workout routine is legendary. He takes 300 shots

a day AFTER his regular practice. This gets upped to 500 shots in the offseason. He does this almost every day, and some estimate he has taken over two million shots over his pro career.

He is great because he gets his reps in.

Lin Mauel Miranda is one of the best Broadway writers and directors to ever exist. He's won a Pulitzer Prize, two Tony awards, two Emmy awards, and five Grammys. His musical Hamilton, telling the story of the Founding Fathers through rap, is the 4th highest-grossing Broadway musical of all time bringing in over $1 billion at the box office. He's written songs for movies ranging from *Moana* and *Encanto* to *Star Wars: The Rise of Skywalker.*

Miranda started early. He began acting and writing in school, and the earliest draft of his first musical *In the Heights* came out during his sophomore year in college. He takes on projects ranging from his famous musicals, to movies, to Sesame Street. Miranda took seven years to write *Hamilton*, admitting he spent a year alone on the song "My Shot."

He is successful because he gets his reps in.

At thirty-one, Bill Gates became the world's youngest billionaire. Between 1995 and 2017, *Forbes Magazine* ranked him as the wealthiest person in the world. The company he founded when he was twenty, Microsoft, dominated the world's computers for decades via the Windows operating system (I am writing this on a computer using it), and it has a market cap of over $3 Trillion. This makes Microsoft the world's 4th most valuable company.

Gates started programming when he was thirteen. Shortly after, he and four classmates formed their first computer club to make money and gain computer time. His high school hired them to program a new class scheduling system, which they did by the time they graduated. He enrolled at Harvard after high school, and immediately took graduate-level computing classes. For the first five years of Microsoft's existence, Gates says he personally reviewed and rewrote every line of computer code the company produced. Even after stepping down as CEO in 2000, he stayed on as their Chief Software Architect.

He became rich because he got his reps in.

Author Malcolm Gladwell wrote about expertise in his book *Outliers: Stories of Success*. In it, he constantly mentions what he calls the "10,000 Hour Rule." Using The Beatles' time in Hamburg as an example, he argues that the key to success in any field is to constantly practice correctly. "It takes 10,000 hours to truly master anything. Time spent leads to experience; experience leads to proficiency; and the more proficient you are the more valuable you'll be."

Merriam Webster's Dictionary defines an expert as "one with the special skill or knowledge representing mastery of a particular subject." This lines up really well with someone who has put in the reps and gotten their 10,000 hours in.

In short, they know what the fuck they are doing.

This seems pretty easy to understand, as who hasn't practiced something for a while and gotten better? I trust my local pizza place to have someone who has the skill to throw dough, so when I order a pie, it comes out right. I trust my local airport to have people with the skill to direct planes, so when I fly somewhere, I don't die. And I trust Angus Young to shred on guitar when I see ACDC in concert.

The War on Expertise

Shared faith in people with years of training and getting their reps in lets us all trust the engineers who designed the cars we drive, the doctors we see when we get sick, and the teachers who educate our kids. Years of experience and education also guide journalists in charge of reporting the news, and the scientists who spend decades learning and researching the world around us. Using the information they provide as a shared basis of understanding is what makes us a great country. We created the light bulb, landed on the moon, invented the internet, and created the first modern government where a diverse population made all of our decisions together without a king.

Unfortunately, in modern society, many men trust experts less and less. Using that internet we invented, everyone can "do their own research" even though much of that information doesn't come from those who've put their reps in. Most of it comes from people who just like talking shit.

In April of 2020, 39% of Americans said they had "a great deal" of trust in scientists while only 12% said "Not too much/No Confidence at all." By October of 2023, that number flipped. Only 23% expressed a lot of trust in scientists while 27% said they didn't.

Vaccines

One of the biggest recent examples of this trend? Vaccines.

Getting a vaccine trains your body to fight disease by introducing weakened or dead versions of bacteria or viruses into your system. While you may get low-level sick for a little while after receiving the vaccine, during that time your body is adapting and building natural defenses so when you get exposed to the real thing, you are already prepared to fight it off.

Vaccination is as American as apple pie. Don't believe me? You know the guy on the $1 Bill? George Washington? He used inoculation, an early form of vaccination, against smallpox to beat the British in the Revolutionary War. He forced all of his troops to do it, saying that smallpox was more destructive to his army "than the sword." It was a huge risk, as many of his soldiers got sick through the process and the British could have attacked while they recovered. But they got better, and by the end of 1777, Washington saw a huge increase in recruitment because of the inoculation effort, which helped us win the war.

You may have never heard of smallpox, but it is one of the most transmittable viruses ever and kills 30% of the people it infects. Modern vaccines have *eliminated it from the planet*. Polio, tetanus, and cholera have all pretty much been terminated from the western world because vaccines for them have been widely distributed. And this isn't all historical. HPV is a virus that causes cervical cancer in women. Since 2016, a vaccine has been available and is super effective with a 97% rate of stopping cancer if you ever get exposed to HPV.

Vaccines work, not by magic but by a fairly simple strategy that even a dumb retired politician like me can explain ...and they have eliminated or reduced some of the worst diseases in the world. It is literally one of the most pro-life things people have ever done.

Which brings us back to now. The internet has allowed

conspiracy theories NOT based in fact to make people question the science of vaccines and the experts who talk about it. Since COVID, we've hit a high point in the number of Americans who view vaccines as more harmful than the diseases they guard against, even though there is no data backing their viewpoints. Popular figures like NFL Quarterback Aaron Rogers refused to get a COVID vaccine when it came out, and even lying about it to the press in 2022. He said his refusal was based on his identity as a "critical thinker" who had "done his own research."

Look, do I trust Rogers in diagnosing a weak side corner blitz and using the situation to hit a streaking receiver over the blitzer in a game winning drive? Absolutely. He has gotten his reps in...*as a football player.*

He's not gotten the same reps in as an immunologist.

The more recent sad example? Measles. It's a disease that spreads fast and can be deadly to kids. Vaccines work on measles. For instance, Clark County, Washington had a measles outbreak in 2019. Unvaccinated kids were asked to stay home from school for three weeks. Only seventy-one total cases were recorded and zero kids died because the vaccinated kids that were in school didn't spread the disease.

However, in 2025 there was a measles outbreak in West Texas. There were 762 cases, with two-thirds of the cases being children. Ninety-nine people were hospitalized and two kids died. (An unvaccinated adult in eastern New Mexico, where it spread, also died). The big difference between 2025 Texas and 2019 Washington state? Health officials say when 95% of any population gets vaccinated, it stops the spread of a disease like measles. In Washington, they had achieved that rate, but some of those Texas counties let vaccination rates slip below that to around 82%.

And kids died.

Critics of vaccination have existed as long as, well, vaccines. Washington had to force his generals to get their troops inoculated for smallpox and examples of these movements include an actual anti-vaccination league in the 1800s and efforts to stop vaccines for diphtheria, pertussis, and tetanus (three other nasty bugs) in the 1970s. The 1990s were when conspiracy theories against the measles vaccine took off.

What are the anti-vaccine arguments here? There seem to be two big ones, and the first one is pretty obvious. Vaccines work best when you get a large amount of the population immune to the disease. When you hit that 95% mark, whatever bug is out there doesn't have the ability to replicate, mutate, and then find new ways of making us sick. That's why there is such a push to get something called "herd immunity" and why the military requires vaccinations. Again, George Washington's legacy.

But people in general, and Americans especially, don't like to be told what to do. And let's face it, getting something injected into your body that might make you feel bad isn't going to be generally popular, even if it is voluntary.

The second reason is skepticism about harm from the vaccines themselves. For measles, there was one British doctor who questioned whether the vaccine caused autism. He didn't say it did, just that it could. The media seized on this and it spread into all sorts of conspiracy theories, even though every credible scientist in the field has shown that it doesn't.

But current U.S. Secretary of Health, RFK Jr., still believes the lies. He hasn't liked vaccines since he went to Samoa in 2019. A couple of kids were killed by improperly prepared vaccines there, and people got scared. He started spreading lies about vaccines and autism. Many listened, and didn't get their kids vaccinated. Eighty-three people, mostly little kids, then died.

Unfortunately, vaccines aren't the only area where people are harmed by a distrust of experts.

Conclusion

RFK Jr. is telling the U.S. government to stop recommending communities put fluoride in their water, even though it is one of the best, cheapest ways to keep Americans' teeth healthy.

37% of Americans believe that God created humans in our present form with no evolution, even though the Catholic Church, of all places, recognizes evolution plays a part in how life develops.

2% of Americans even still believe the world is flat, even though they watch sporting events in different time zones that only happen if the planet is, you know, a globe.

Look, experts are NOT perfect. Health care folks can be overly conservative in approving new and different treatments, hormone therapy and psychedelics to treat PTSD being two big examples. Academics can be hugely insulated and defensive about their work, defending it even if new evidence comes out showing they are wrong.

Furthermore, these things are really complicated and sometimes there is no easy answer. During COVID, New Mexico's death rate was terrible. Native American reservations were decimated, and in my hometown there were so many dead bodies, the local hospital had refrigerated trailers brought in because the morgue was overflowing. So the Governor had some of the longest, hardest shutdowns in the nation. This is an entirely reasonable thing to have done.

Some studies show, though, that states that kept in person schools open longer had better performance than states and districts that kept learning remote for fear of the virus spreading. I am sure their Governors would point to that data as a defense for their actions, and they too have a point.

Furthermore, we all make mistakes...even people who put their reps in. The Beatles had some mediocre songs, Curry doesn't win a title every year, and when Microsoft introduced Windows 95, it had bugs for years.

I mean, George Lucas put Jar Jar into a *Star Wars* movie. Those of us that were around sure remember that flub.

But, let me ask you a question: Do you know what it takes to make a hit movie, or design a new computer operating system? Can you hit a three-pointer with a 7-foot crazy man coming at you as fast as possible? Can you design the engine on a commercial airplane or a health care response plan to a major pandemic?

Maybe a few of you can answer "yes" to one of these questions, but I sure as hell don't have the ability. Furthermore, I cannot fix a major plumbing problem in my house, design a winning investment strategy for a billion-dollar company, or operate a major milk dairy. Could I do some of these if I got an education and years of reps? Maybe. But if I don't, until then I will tend to trust the people that have become experts to do their damn job.

I hope we can all start doing this better as well.

CHAPTER 32

Listening

As I mentioned in the intro, in 2008, I ran for Congress. I had been elected at twenty-five to my local County Commission, thought I had done pretty well, and didn't agree with the guy who was in there. I ended up losing in a primary by 3.5% to a millionaire who gave himself hundreds of thousands of dollars. This was pretty good, except close doesn't count except in horseshoes and hand grenades.

I learned a lesson from the loss, though. In Silver City, New Mexico, right before election day, I ran into a woman I'd met numerous times. When I asked for her support, she told me she already voted for the other guy early. I was stunned. I'd worked my ass off up there, and she was definitely more aligned politically with me than the other guy. When I asked her why, she told me something that I carry with me to this day.

"Every time you came up here, you would shake my hand and then move on to meet the next person. Harry (the guy I ran against) only came up here once, but when he talked to me, *he listened.*"

It's some wisdom I should have gotten into my head eight years earlier. See, I worked at a summer camp for a couple of years called Seeds of Peace. It brought teenagers in from Israel and Palestine, as well as India/Pakistan, North and South Cyprus, and the Balkans. You know, places where people tend to not like each other very much. I taught archery and swing dancing (not at the same time), and most of the kids' time was spent on normal camp stuff like that.

However, these kids were asked to go into a ninety-minute facilitation session every day with a professional to talk about their shit. Those emotional conversations would sometimes extend out past those designated times out into the athletics fields and get pretty hot and heavy.

When that would happen, Tim Wilson would roll up. The camp director, he'd spent decades in western Pennsylvania as a football coach. His knees were shot, so he drove around in a golf cart. When kids would go at it without acknowledging the other person, he'd drive over, stick his finger out in a "get over here" motion obvious to everyone who's had a coach, and say: "Listen up. I'm going to tell you something my momma always told me. God gave you two of these (pointing to his ears) and one of these (pointing to his mouth). And he did it for a reason."

In all that work he did with kids, he learned something important. People want to be heard, and understanding between folks starts with paying attention to each other. Talking over them or trying to prove your suffering means more than theirs doesn't do the job.

And fellas, we can sometimes be bad at this.

Men are from Mars

In his book *Men Are From Mars, Women Are From Venus*, Dr. John Gray shares some of the lessons he learned from decades of couples counseling. The biggest difference between men and women? We talk to each other differently when we have problems.

Men tend to view problematic conversations as a chance to repair something. He actually used the term "Mr. Fix It" as a description for dudes who respond to issues with possible solutions, thinking they are being helpful.

Women though? Many times women aren't having a conversation to solve their problems. They simply want to be heard, recognized, and have their emotions validated. When dudes try to offer suggestions on how to make the situation better, we sometimes bulldoze over women who just want to be listened to thoughtfully.

And fellas, I am a gold star example of this. You already saw my tendency to do this cost me a vote. Then, in my only long-term relationship, there were multiple times during dinner when my partner would talk to me and I would be looking away. She asked me if I was listening to her and I would literally repeat back the last two or three sentences she spoke, thinking I was showing her that I was. But that wasn't what she wanted. She wanted me to engage with her emotionally and validate her experience. That took me a while to figure out. But when I did, things got better.

Listening at Work

Brian Mandell was my Negotiation professor when I was

a student at Harvard. A really smart guy, he would throw around words like ZOPA (Zone of Potential Agreement) and BATNA (Best Alternative to Negotiated Agreement) in this monotone that our class found hilarious.

But the best thing I learned from Professor Mandell's class is that in any negotiation, the absolute most important thing is to *keep asking why*. Why does a person feel this is of value? How do they get there? What can I give them to get this thing done, and why do they want it so bad? If they don't want to talk, why? Do they just not like the person they have to deal with?

Asking lots of questions and listening deeply to the answers helps you get deals over the line in ways that benefit everybody.

How To Win Friends and Influence People was published in 1936, and still might be one of the best books for work you will ever read. Author Dale Carnegie argues that the most important skill is developing relationships, and the best strategy to get someone interested in you is to show interest in them. That means you have to remember their name, give honest appreciation for their time and experience, and deeply listen so you can determine what they really want.

Without truly hearing someone else, you will never really know them and have a hard time forming a bond that might benefit you both.

Interrupting and Mansplaining

When men talk to men, we tend to listen. When women talk to women, they tend to listen. But when men talk to ladies? We interrupt them. This happens at work quite a bit, but also occurs in cafes, drug stores, and university campuses. Why? Deborah Tannen has spent decades studying how both genders communicate, and finds that men generally use speaking as a way to assert control over a situation, whereas women are socialized to talk as a way to connect with another person.

Put in simpler terms, men use report talk while women use rapport talk. It is similar to the conclusion Gray found in *Men Are from Mars*. Guys want to solve problems, and use our conversational time to assert control over our surroundings to get things done.

Sometimes, though, men can be just dicks about this. Probably the most prominent public example happened in 2009. Kanye West barged on stage as Taylor Swift was giving her winner's speech at the Video Music Awards, ripping the mic out of her hand to rant about how Beyoncé should have won. Swift left the stage without completing her speech, only for Beyoncé later to invite her up to finish. Unfortunately, the kind of attitude Kanye displayed leads to another problem.

Ever hear of the term "mansplaining"? If you haven't, talk to almost any woman and she'll tell you. Our "report talk" and need to control a conversation can devolve into us talking down to women and trying to describe or explain something to her, whether she wants us to or not. Lots of times she already knows what is going on but we haven't bothered to ask her.

When we mansplain, we can come across as rude dicks. This has consequences.

If you do it at work with female coworkers, they will probably feel like you don't value them and be less likely to speak up even when their input is sorely needed. If you have a female partner and do this shit regularly at home? Well, that's the kind of thing that will either have you sleeping on the couch or getting back on the dating apps soon.

When we interrupt or mansplain, we don't listen and therefore lose the ability to know the "why" in a negotiation setting. This makes it harder to get deals done.

And Dale Carnegie would say it stops you from establishing good relationships. "Listen first. Give your opponents a chance to talk. Let them finish. Do not resist, defend or debate. This only raises barriers."

Maybe most importantly, if we get a reputation for not listening, people won't ask us for help. And most men, myself included, want to be seen as problem solvers.

Conclusion

I have a lawyer friend who once told me the American legal system is based on structured contests between opposing sides. In this case, a conflict decided upon by a judge or jury to settle a problem is good. But he said he sometimes gets frustrated as more and more women lawyers enter the profession. In his view, they want to avoid conflict. He said sometimes they listen so much, they forget that the point isn't to establish an emotional connection, but to get to a solution.

And he has a point.

There are definitely times and places where decisive action and straight talk are needed. In football, a quarterback has to have the ability to call out plays and formations quickly and players had better follow their directions. The same thing can be said of a crisis situation, like a flood or after a crime, where leaders don't have time for long discussions in order to solve the problem.

However, fellas, many of us do interrupt regularly. We sometimes only listen to develop our own argument to "win" a discussion. When we do, it can make us less likely to accomplish stuff at work or at home, and keep us from establishing the relationships that lead to healthy and happy lives.

So maybe do like I did eventually (but too late to win that election) and take a lesson from Tim Wilson: Remember, God gave you two ears and one mouth...for a reason.

CHAPTER 33

Sexuality

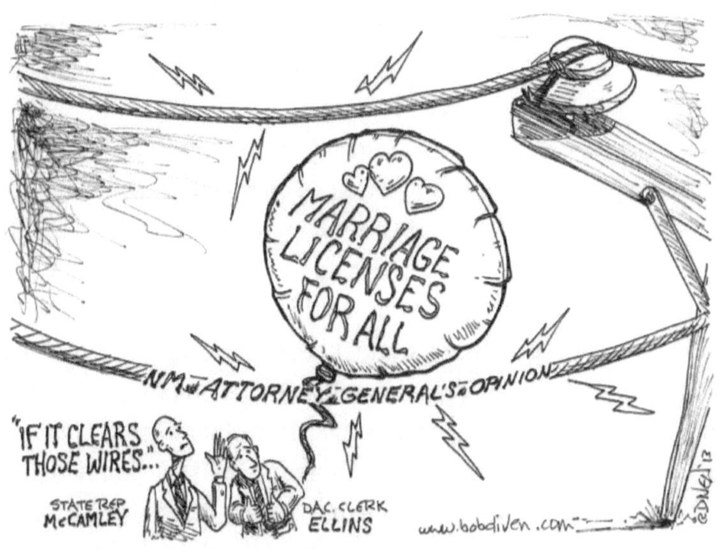

Political Cartoon provided courtesy of artist Bob Diven

I am a pretty conventional straight dude. Growing up, I never had any doubt about my attraction to women, nor any internal question about my manhood.

As awkward as my middle and high school years were, though, this was good because as a guy, the worst thing you could be called by other dudes was "gay," "homo," or a "fag." Those insults were thrown around cheaply in the lunchroom, classes, and athletic fields to tell someone they were weak. In the '80s and '90s, we didn't know too many, if any, folks that were openly out.

Hell, the first time I saw two dudes holding hands was outside of my college student union in 1998.

While people with different sexual preferences are much more accepted now, I still see men online using the same old stupid insults. Research shows that men, especially men living in rural communities, use them regularly. And men are less likely than women to think gay marriage should be legal and is morally OK. I mean, just look at who watches *Heated Rivalry*. Hint...It's all women.

Even so, we've come a long way in our country on this issue and one of the first big changes came when I was a kid.

In 1994, President Bill Clinton made a new rule called "Don't Ask, Don't Tell." Basically, it said if you were gay but didn't talk about it you wouldn't be discharged from military service. This was hugely controversial, as since the Revolutionary War, being homosexual meant you got the boot. In World War II and afterwards, military brass treated it as a psychological disorder. This remained the policy until Clinton, with almost 17,000 people getting discharged in the 1980s alone. One of the best examples to show how people thought of gay troops came from a TV show.

*M*A*S*H** was one of the most popular shows in American history. It began airing in the waning days of Vietnam as a darkly funny take on war, portraying a group of doctors in a Mobile Army Surgical Hospital (MASH) unit during the Korean Conflict. I was only a little kid when the last episode aired in 1983, but remembered people talking about it as it remains the highest-rated non-Super Bowl U.S. show ever.

One of the characters, Sergeant Klinger, had a recurring bit. He'd been drafted, didn't want to be there, and was trying to get declared mentally unfit for military service and be sent home. The various hijinks he tried included eating an entire Jeep, pretending to think he was a camel driver, and wearing a rubber suit and fur coat during a heat wave.

The thing the character is most remembered for is constantly dressing like a woman. He wanted to be called crazy, not actually labeled gay. *M*A*S*H** treated Klinger gently, making fun of how American culture historically handled anyone who wasn't a traditionally straight person as insane and unwanted. But that was nothing new.

History

Sodomy laws banning anal sex were first brought from England to Virginia in 1610, New York in 1613, and Massachusetts in 1632. They were hardly ever enforced early on, and records show only three people were ever convicted in the colonies. But they remained on the books after the Revolution until the 1960s.

Interestingly, anti-gay laws always focused on men. Women's relationships with one another were fairly common, with the term "Boston Marriages" used to describe long term female couples who never married guys. For years, women were not seen as having any sexual desire, so there was no threat to traditional marriage from their being together.

One of the catalysts to changing these laws was a 1969 New York City riot. The Greenwich Village Stonewall Inn was one of the few places where gay folks could dance. While the police commonly conducted raids they were usually on weekdays, and the Mafia owners were alerted beforehand. In July of '69, though, the "Police Morals Squad" staged a raid early on a Saturday morning when there was a packed house. Bar patrons and others gathered to watch, and after one of the people arrested resisted and was hit on the head with a baton the crowd outside overturned cars, set fires, and fought with the cops.

Riots continued throughout the week, and peaceful protests soon followed. Stonewall is still seen as a watershed moment for the LGBT community with thousands of organizations formed in the years after. The reason that Pride parades are held late in the summer is to mark the anniversary of the riots.

Reforms to anti-sodomy laws started when Illinois repealed its version in 1961. Spurred on by Stonewall, twenty other states followed in the '70s. After a six-year discussion in California, State Senate majority leader George Moscone kept a deadlocked state Senate open for hours in 1975 until the Lt. Governor could fly back to the Capitol in a private plane and cast the deciding vote to repeal their version.

Moscone later became the mayor of San Francisco. He was a proponent of the city's first Gay Rights Ordinance in 1978 along with Harvey Milk, a newly elected city councilman and one of the first openly gay elected officials in the country. Both Moscone and Milk were assassinated later that year by the only city councilor to vote against it.

In the '90s, "Don't Ask, Don't Tell" was seen as a sort of step forward, but also by many as a betrayal as it forced servicemembers to live a secret double life. In 1996, conservative lawmakers passed the Defense of Marriage Act, which said that the U.S. government couldn't recognize same-sex marriage, and that a same-sex married couple wouldn't have their marriage recognized in a state where it wasn't legal. And in 1998, Matthew Shepard, a twenty-one year-old gay student in Wyoming, was brutally beaten with a pistol and left in a coma tied to a farm fence for eighteen hours before he died.

This is the time when I started being, in my own small way, involved in this stuff.

Homecoming Queen

My start in politics came in 1998 when I was elected to the student Senate at New Mexico State University. The next fall, this kid named Aaron Schubert ran for Homecoming Queen as a man. The LGBT community on campus got really excited, as this was a chance for them to be really involved for the first time openly. Aaron ended up getting enough votes for 2nd Princess, meaning he was in the parade and got an introduction at the football game.

I didn't know Aaron at the time, but my friend and former dorm supervisor Demetrius was elected as 2nd Prince representing the Black Student Union. D is a big, tough former high school football player and I didn't know how he would feel about teaming up with Schubert. When I asked him, though, he just laughed and said, "Man it's all good. We'll have fun!" They put a rainbow flag on the back of their car for the parade, smiled and waved, and everyone ended up having a good time.

Some, though, didn't like it and brought a bill before the student Senate. It said to run for King, you had to be a man and for Queen, a woman. The debate was deep and personal. The sponsors used the word "tradition" a lot, saying that Homecoming wasn't a place to make "political statements." Schubert and the LGBT folks, on the other hand, argued that in their community guys were elected Queens all the time and that he got enough votes for the position. Therefore the restriction would limit democracy in future elections. It made all sorts of national news, and ended up passing by a single vote.

Though I had never been involved in these types of issues before, I got really invested. I met all of these gay people for the first time, and found them not to be characters or stereotypes I'd seen portrayed in the media. They were real folks who loved the school, had feelings like everyone else, and were thrilled to be included in a big-time University event for the first time. I argued their point passionately, but when the bill passed, their disappointment was palpable. It was like a door had just opened a crack and now was slamming shut in their faces. The whole thing was just shitty.

It turned out OK, though. I became President the year after, and appointed a Supreme Court chief who overturned that law on the basis of equality and democracy. Aaron got elected to the Senate, went on to get married in 2013, and built a great career in public health around the world. And a couple of years ago, the name of the court was changed from "King and Queen" to Royalty.

No one gets hurt and everyone can now feel included in the ceremonies.

Marriage Equality

In 2013, after serving in my first session as a New Mexico State Representative, I got a call from the local County Clerk. The issue of marriage equality was being tied up at the state Supreme Court, who didn't seem to want to deal with it. I knew the Clerk, Lynn Ellins, well. He was a lawyer by trade and he told me he agreed with an interpretation that the NM Constitution didn't actually have gender in the marriage part of the document. So he wanted to push the issue by marrying some folks and forcing the Court to make a decision.

I replied that I thought it was a great idea, but why the hell was he calling me? It turns out he wanted to get an official opinion from the Attorney General, but only a legislator could make the ask. I told him to give me an hour to get a shower and put on a suit and I would be right over.

We sent the letter and waited three months for the response. It turns out the AG, like the Supreme Court, didn't want to touch it. Therefore, I worked with the Clerk and his staff during the summer to plan a day where we would just start marrying people and dare anyone to stop it. My job was to raise money for the eventual lawsuit (which never ended up happening) and find ten couples who would be willing to get married.

The trick? We had to keep it secret because we wanted to get the licenses issued before we might get stopped. So I met with a bunch of people in the LGBT community, heard about some likely couples, and the Wednesday afternoon before our target day I made a bunch of calls that went something like this, "Hi, my name is Bill, and I am one of your local State Reps. You may not know me, and please don't tell anyone... but would you like to get married tomorrow? If so, we need you to be at the Clerk's office at 8:00 a.m. on the nose."

The next morning, we had those couples ready to go. The first two were Frank and Paul, who had been together for thirty years. My mom is their friend and agreed to be their witness. Word spread quickly, and by lunchtime we had almost sixty couples married. A lesbian duo drove the forty miles up from Ft. Bliss in Texas so fast that one of the brides didn't even change out of her uniform.

I have never in my life, before or since, been in a room so full of life and joy. The laughter was loud, the smiles were wide, and there were so many exclamations of "Holy Shit! I never thought this would happen!"

It was the single best thing I ever did as a public official.

What's the Problem?

I say all of that to say this: To the dudes who still have a problem with LGBTQ folks? Honestly, what's the problem here? How are they a threat to you? If you're uncomfortable with the thought of two same-sex people getting down, fine. But they aren't doing it in public, and there are certainly no laws forcing you to participate. So how does their being happy honestly affect you in any way?

Trans people are more the issue of the day because for many of us, it's a relatively new phenomenon and tough to get our head around. One of the most effective ads in the 2024 campaign was "Kamala is for They/Them. Trump is for You!" We know by now all of the attention from the left for women has many dudes feeling abandoned. Trump's ads hit that emotion hard, and were even more effective because it compares men's struggles to the issues of people going through something we have no clue how to understand.

But again, how does it affect you? Some say they worry about men dressing up as women just to go into women's bathrooms. This is not only super rare, there is zero evidence that more men try it after laws allowing trans women to use women's bathrooms get passed. And male custodians go into women's bathrooms all the time, so if a man wanted to commit assault, he could easily do so without risking ridicule or harassment by appearing as a woman.

And let's talk about trans girls in sports. The argument is that men who transition to be women are so physically dominant that they steal women's scholarships. But that ALMOST NEVER HAPPENS. The NCAA in 2024 had over 510,000 athletes in their various sports at all levels. At a U.S. Senate panel when this issue came up, the NCAA Commissioner said there were fewer than ten total trans athletes. That's .0002%. He didn't talk about the ratio of men vs women or where they played, but only two of the ten were trans women playing in high-level sports, a swimmer and a volleyball player.

In high schools, the numbers are even sillier. In 2023, when the Ohio state legislature brought up a law to ban trans athletes (passed in 2024), they scoured the state of eight million people to find examples they could use. *They found one playing varsity sports.* Her name? Ember Zelch. In an interview with journalist Pablo Torre, she described her situation as the third string catcher on her softball team.

She wasn't any good, never hit a home run, just joined because she wanted to play, and no one on her team (or anyone else's) seemed to care.

Again, fellas, no one is being hurt here.

On this issue, Dwayne Wade probably said it best. You'll know him from his three NBA championship rings, thirteen appearances in the All-Star game, and his 2008 gold medal (where he led the Dream Team in scoring). He's also the father of a trans daughter, and the only thing he has ever expressed about her is love and support. "I don't put anything on [my kids] because of maybe the worldly view of how I'm 'supposed' to look at someone or what I think someone should be, because if I did that, then I wouldn't be where I'm at today," he says. "I think I'm lucky to have them and I think they're lucky to have me."

The Story is an Old One

We've been better about this stuff recently. Gay marriage was legalized nationally by the Supreme Court in 2015, and it refused to reverse this decision in November of 2025. The Defense of Marriage Act was repealed by Congress in 2022 and openly gay service members had zero effect on military units' readiness, morale, or cohesion after the repeal of "Don't Ask, Don't Tell."

In 2021, Las Vegas Raider Carl Nasib became the first openly gay player in the NFL. No one seemed to give a fuck, and in his first game as an out man the edge rusher strip-sacked Ravens QB Lamar Jackson, leading to the winning touchdown in a playoff season.

But it ain't all wine and roses. Assaults, harassment,

and threats of LGBTQ folks were actually up in 2024. They also report higher rates of discrimination in health care and homelessness. Gay teens are still more likely to commit suicide than their straight peers, and petty Pete Hegseth recently stripped the Navy ship USS Harvey Milk of its name during Pride Month because he wants to promote "Warrior Culture."

Uh huh.

After he died, my mom found a copy of a letter my old man wrote to the local chapter of the Retired Officers Association. They were trying to get him to join up in the early '90s, and were using opposition to "Don't Ask, Don't Tell" as a recruiting tool. His reply did not fuck around.

> Please remove my name from your mailing list. I do not intend to apply for membership in the Mesilla Valley Chapter of TROA. This will save you the time and trouble that it takes to send me the monthly mailing.
>
> I did consider joining but...your March mailing included a proliferation of 'ACT NOW TO BAN HOMO-SEXUALS FROM THE ARMED FORCES,' a narrow-minded and ignorant 900 letter pitch. This bigoted action smacks of paranoia and narcissism. I can only pray to God to forgive such a blatantly immoral, judgmental, and self-righteous action that reeks of fanatical intolerance coupled with unfounded fear of the unknown. This mind-set is the exact same one that was and is against Negroes and women serving throughout the armed services because they will be a 'detriment to discipline and morale' and of course,

they will drastically reduce READINESS. The story is an old one but the sickness remains the same.

PLEASE REMOVE MY NAME FROM YOUR MAILING LIST

Michael E. McCamley

LTC, USA (RET)

1993

Choose smiles and love over slamming doors in people's faces. It's the manly thing to do.

CHAPTER 34

Interviews with Interesting Guys
CAMRIN BLAKE

Camrin is a "retired" man.

A trans woman, she grew up in a conservative environment that focused on traditional masculinity. Pushing feelings down throughout school that she didn't quite understand, she looked for the most "manly" things she could do. So before transitioning, she spent over three years in the 3rd Air Wing of the U.S. Marine Corps when she identified as a man.

After getting out of the Corps, she decided to prioritize her mental health, which meant finally taking the step of transitioning to the gender she knew she always was. Putting a team of counselors and doctors together, she began and is now continuing her transition while studying for her Bachelor's Degree in History.

She likes jean jackets, has an extensive guitar collection, and likes her heavy metal. She is also willing to share what her experience is like as a trans woman for people that have never looked into what that process really means.

Being a Man

"My dad was a strong male role model in my life. He was active duty in the Air Force from sometime in the '90s all the way up to 2018, so basically my entire life up until graduating high school. After I entered middle school, I started to kind of explore mentally this idea of gender identity without really knowing what it was. It's not something you know right off the bat, you're like, 'Oh, I'm trans.' You feel like you're just wrong. Some people, they feel wrong right away. Some people, it's like, 'Oh, I just, I wish I was born a girl. I wish I looked like a woman.' But that's normal. And then, you ask people and talk about it, and you realize 'Oh, shit, like, no one else has this. No one else around me quite feels the same way.' You start hearing slurs about trans people and, and it ingrained this idea that that part of me was bad and wrong. And so, I just shoved it down with a big stick into my psyche for a while. And so, from high school onwards, I really focused on trying to be as masculine as possible. This is very common in trans people.

"And that probably played into why I joined the Marine Corps, because that's the most masculine branch, you know? It's your knucklehead, knuckle-dragger, door-kicker thing. I was like, 'Yeah, that's masculine. That's what I want to do.' Military family and I didn't want to pay for college because I sucked at school. I was doing bad in high school. So I was like, 'I can just join the military. I'll be fine.'"

Life in the Corps

"It was pretty rough. You know, I worked with a lot of great dudes. But you start to get to know them personally and understand their beliefs. You have some people who are a lot more accepting than others, and you have some that are extremely the opposite...very radically not accepting people. This was also the same time I finally started to actually explore taking care of my mental health and going to therapy. I went to rehab because I had a major drinking problem when I was in the Marine Corps, and I took it too far.

"I realized that this thing was weighing on me and it was crushing. It's like I'm having to act as an entirely different person every single day, not only to coworkers but my family and my closest friends. I'm trying to convince every single person, including me, that I'm not me. And it sucks. And so eventually, I got out in December of 2021. September of that year is when I came out to my family and my closest friends but I was kind of biding my time to come out socially until I got out of the Marine Corps because that was just, like, not a safe environment.

"When I came out later socially early that next year, probably, like, 75%, 80% of the shop that I used to work with cut contact with me. So yeah. That's why I wanted to wait until I got out...to come out socially, because I was just unsafe."

Process of Transition

"Overall, it took almost two years for me to get started on

medication because I had to convince people that I was trans. Medical providers' first instinct is to not believe you and when it comes to a lot of mental health stuff, including gender identity, they boil it down to, like you know, 'Is this, like, a sexual fetish for you?' It gets really demeaning at parts, especially near the beginning until you actually have a good team. In between those two years, I was still figuring out myself. How do I want to dress? How do I want to be perceived? I kind of overcompensated the other way, becoming a lot more hyperfeminine because I had never really been in that area."

Medication

"I'm getting my brain, my nervous system accustomed to an entirely separate hormonal blueprint. Because your brain has the blueprints of how to utilize both testosterone and estrogen. And so when you suppress testosterone and introduce estrogen, the blueprint's already there. It knows what to do with that hormone, and it just goes with it. It just takes some time to get used to it. So, you essentially are going through another puberty."

Dealing with Violence

"At the end of last year, I went to the bar with a few friends, all queer folk. These are two people that are a bit smaller, daintier than me so I was like their helicopter mom for the night, making sure that they were safe. I've dealt with, like, both just, like, verbal and physical violence from bigots so I'd rather have a bit of a buffer. So someone was harassing my two friends and I put myself between them, and asked the bartender and the bouncer to kick him out and we enjoyed the rest of our night. We spent about another hour and a half, two hours in the bar and after we left, the dude that was just previously kicked out was still waiting out there.

"We come outside, and he's still nowhere near sober. He starts walking towards us and I put myself between my two friends because I thought this guy was just going to get up in our face and yell at us. He shoved me and pulled out a knife, but I tackled him to the ground and he stabbed me in the chest. I did end up having to go to the hospital for that. I had a punctured right lung which I don't know if, if you've ever had a lung reinflated, it sucks. That sucks more than, like, a catheter. And I was lucky, you know? I'm glad that I was there because like it could have been a lot worse for the other two people that were there. It was, you know, I kind of sobered up immediately in those like five seconds.

"There are people who get assaulted every day. They get beaten and killed or thrown out of their homes when they're like sixteen. So I did escape that in not too rough of a shape in comparison to what could have been. Because that is something we have to expect and prepare for every single day just to live our lives. How bizarre it is to look back and say, 'Oh, I'm glad I only got a punctured lung.'"

A Request

"Just try to get out of whatever echo chamber that you're in, because it's very easy to get into and be stuck into an echo chamber online. Just go out and talk to someone. Humanize the people around you rather than, like, see them as these faceless evil creatures. Like, I'm in a metal band. I'm a big country fan. I have eleven guitars total. I'll probably get a few more. I like having them even though they all do the same exact thing."

The Bottom Line

Social media has eroded any kind of complexity and nuance in our conversations. 280-character tweets and 15-60 second short videos lack the ability to truly explain how thick and thorny some situations are. Combine that with systems that promote anger to generate clicks and a focus on owning the other side, and we lose the ability to truly understand how to make things better for ourselves and the people around us.

This is certainly a main issue for how we act as guys, and it's anything but simple. A solution to all of this, though, is to better understand each other by putting ourselves in each other's shoes.

For the Gentlemen

Fellas, I get it. Many of us don't know what to do right now. On the one hand, we're told to move over because people like us have had control for so long, and that many of the things we think we're good at aren't wanted anymore.

On the other hand, if we aren't seen as supportive enough to others or try to reasonably talk about the problems we are legitimately having, we get shut down with anger and derision from the same people.

Basically pass the mic to someone else AND silence about others is complicity. It can be so, so fucking frustrating.

But do me a favor, and put yourself in the shoes of the ladies out there. Many of them, especially older women, grew up in an era where they were told by almost everyone to raise kids and otherwise get out of the way. Women today are still facing a ton of challenges:

- Sexual harassment claims at work are up, with the over 7,700 complaints at the EEOC, the highest amount in over a decade.
- Ladies are still assaulted at an alarming rate. As many as 41% of women have had a domestic assault in their lifetime, with over ten million experiencing some kind of partner violence every year.
- In a recent report, women in the workplace are saying they're less interested in being promoted than men, not because they are less motivated, but because they don't feel as much support at their companies.
- As we've mentioned previously, the current Secretary of Defense reposts videos saying women should lose

the right to vote, and the U.S. Speaker of the House faces criticism because he refuses to put Republican women in leadership positions. Meanwhile, the influential conservative Heritage Foundation recently hired a dude into their leadership who believes that employers should "support traditional family life by hiring only male heads of households."

- In spite of all of this, polls show that women are now valuing their careers, financial independence, and mental health over relationships. Conservative men, and this is most of us as the majority voted for Trump, have different priorities. Men want to get married and have kids, but value emotional stability as the least of their priorities. This frustrates so many women.
- Though improving, women (even if they make more money in a relationship) still do way more of the domestic work around the house than their male partners.

With all of that, it seems pretty easy to understand why many ladies have a lot of rage and frustration about us fellas right now. They deserve real, significant places in all levels of our society without having to fear that men will constantly interrupt, ignore, and assault them. If we refuse to treat them as trusted and equal co-workers, partners, lovers, and friends, that only fuels those feelings.

Telling them to submit to husbands or get back to the kitchen sure isn't the solution.

For the Ladies

After I printed the chapter questioning whether the

political left really wants straight men in their coalitions, I received a ton of feedback from women on various social media sites. The following quotes represent the type of reactions I got:

- *"Men ARE the problem."*
- *"We want you to say it with us that men as a whole are terrible."*
- *"You won't catch me worrying about men's mental health again."*
- *"Yes, men, and yes, statistically straight white men ARE the problem."*
- *"You've lost your seat at the table."* (this one was to me specifically)
- *"I love the male loneliness epidemic because it's only happening to shitty men and shitty men can't stand that."*

Ladies, I hear you. For all the reasons described above, I appreciate where you might be coming from. But I respectfully, and strongly, disagree with these statements.

Most men are NOT terrible. We are not just problems to solve, but real people with feelings and ambitions who deserve help and representation. In democracies, everyone should have a seat at the table, and asking us to completely erase ourselves, as some feminists suggest, isn't going to work.

So do me a favor, and put yourself in our shoes and see some of the things we are observing about the world around us:

- Many of us see an education system weighted against us, with more suspensions and expulsions for boys, fewer male teachers to provide role models, more girls graduating high school, being named valedictorians, and more scholarship opportunities for women, even though they are currently dominating both current college enrollment and graduation rates.
- We see places for men to gather and talk (like union halls, barbershops, and bars) disappearing, while women seem to retain many places to gather (business associations, the YWCA, Girl Scouts, etc.).
- Many of us are confused about or scared of talking to women. Instead, we turn to porn and AI to scratch that itch, even though doing so doesn't make us happy in the long run.
- Many of us think that feminism exists not to just elevate women, but to tear men down. A straight male friend of mine messaged me during the same conversation from above to express this thought. "...feminist women disregard our pain, our issues. We as men have changed so much since the time of our parents. We've become what they've 'asked' us to become and yet they still want to dismiss us."
- We are killing ourselves, ending up on the street, getting addicted, and are imprisoned at much higher rates than women.

The term "walking on eggshells" comes up all the time when men discuss how we communicate with women. This constant worry about how to react creates the anger, frustration, and loneliness that lead many guys to turn to the likes of

Andrew Tate or conservative religious leaders, who seem to be the only people willing to validate male existence.

Physical strength, risk taking, a want to protect and provide, and being tough are things many men are proud of. They can also be forces for good if we can learn to be better listeners, more honest with our emotions, and understand that we don't need to control everything around us all the time to define ourselves.

Please join us in recognizing that.

Not a Zero-Sum Game

In the chapter on men and listening, I talked about my experience working at Seeds of Peace camp at the turn of the century. Those kids coming from war zones all shared a trait in common. They thought that if they acknowledged another group's pain or troubles in any way, that understanding would somehow lessen their own situation. So they shied away from it, engaging in a "comparison of suffering" that made learning where the other side came from really tough.

In economics, this is called a zero sum game. It means that in any situation with two groups, when one gains the other has to lose. This seems a very accurate way to describe how many talk about gender today. Many women see any kind of help for men, with the associated time and money needed to make it work, as taking away resources from their own efforts at equality. Meanwhile many men, especially young ones, see the efforts to create space, help, and support women as not being available in the same ways to them. Since so many are having problems, it makes them feel like they are losing.

But it doesn't have to be this way.

Things We Can Do

There are some great examples of efforts to help men that don't take away from creating a more equitable world for the ladies.

The school district in Austin, TX created the Gus Garcia Young Men's Leadership Academy. It's an all-boys middle school with over 250 students who mostly come from homes where a male role model isn't present. More than half the teachers are men, and one third are African American, giving these boys the types of mentors they may not have in their daily lives.

In Maryland, where only 23% of teachers are men, the state recently allocated $19M to recruit more men into the classroom through non-traditional pathways. The goal is to increase diversity in a profession where men are rare, which then creates better educational outcomes for boys.

Another good effort is on the other coast in California. The state is partnering with five organizations, including Big Brothers, the YMCA, and the San Francisco Giants Foundation to help recruit 10,000 young men to fill needed mentor positions and address young men's issues with "disconnection, loneliness, and lack of direction."

Construction trade unions, where membership is over 90% male, is second only to the mining industry in suicide rate. To help combat this and create better mental health, many Unions have or are thinking about creating programs that encourage their members to get trained and act as peer support for their co-workers. The goal is to have members with mental health problems lean into their teammates and get help personally, while also having the option to talk to union paid-for professional councilors who can help them work through their shit.

Non-profit groups are also doing good work here. Barack Obama's My Brother's Keeper Alliance focuses on education and employment for young men of color, providing things like scholarships and leadership training. And the Movember Foundation, which originally started to bring awareness to prostate and testicular cancer, has expanded their activities to include mental health, fatherhood, and overall quality of life for dudes.

All of these efforts are needed, positive, and build more resources to help men through our obvious issues WITHOUT taking away needed programs for women. We should support them.

A Final Message

My brothers, I know times are tough right now for many of us. We may be struggling financially, emotionally, in our relationships, with our health, and sometimes even with our reasons for being alive. Some on the right tell us the only way out of this is to "dominate," while some on the left tell us to withdraw. Neither are correct.

But there is a middle ground, and we can thread this needle.

Therefore, I issue a challenge to you on some simple things:

Get the fuck offline, and into the real world once in a

while. ChatGPT and online girlfriends will not make us happier, healthier people. But real friends, family, support networks, and, yeah, even actual girlfriends and wives can make us more complete people. Seek them out, and work to keep them around.

Let's deal with our mental health. By being more honest with ourselves and the people around us, by admitting when we feel joy or sadness, stress or fulfillment, energized and exhausted, and acceptance or rejection we can be better, more grounded men. Life is better than not living, but we've got to work to accept that.

Set time aside for exercise, sleeping, getting outside, cleaning your house, and making sure you eat right. These little things will make you feel better, and the women in your life will appreciate them, as well.

Let's get our financial houses in order by choosing careers where we know jobs will be around, and by committing to getting the education needed to get and keep them. When our bank accounts are put in order by doing fulfilling work, we can celebrate true accomplishment.

Treat women like the complete, real people that they are, and when you find one you can trust, don't hold back from being your true self around her. She will truly appreciate the connection, and these female friendships will make you a better person.

Thanks so much for taking the time to read this. I can tell you, as someone who is trying to take all of this advice as well, that we can be happier, healthier, better, and most importantly...alive.

Keep your heads up out there y'all.